Thank You for My Service

Thank You for My Service

MAT BEST

with

Ross Patterson & Nils Parker

Bantam Books
New York

The views expressed in this publication are those of the author
and do not necessarily reflect the official policy and position of the Department
of Defense or the U.S. Government. The public release clearance of this
publication by the Department of Defense does not imply the Department of
Defense endorsement or factual accuracy of the material.

Some names, identifying characteristics, and other details
have been changed to protect the privacy of the individuals involved.
In some cases, composite characters have been created for the purpose
of further disguising the identity of individuals. Finally, in some instances,
the author rearranged and/or compressed events and time periods
in service of the narrative.

Published in the United States by Bantam Books, an imprint of
Random House, a division of Penguin Random House LLC, New York.

BANTAM BOOKS and the HOUSE colophon are registered trademarks
of Penguin Random House LLC.

LIBRARY OF CONGRESS CATALOGING-IN-PUBLICATION DATA

Names: Best, Mat, author.
Title: Thank you for my service / Mat Best.
Description: First edition. | New York: Bantam Books, [2019]
Identifiers: LCCN 2019016176 (print) | LCCN 2019020166 (ebook) |
ISBN 9781524796501 (Ebook) | ISBN 9781524796495 (hardcover)
Subjects: LCSH: Best, Mat. | Veterans—United States—Biography. |
United States. Army. Ranger Regiment, 75th Battalion, 2nd—
Biography. | Iraq War, 2003–2011—Personal narratives, American. |
Afghan War, 2001—Personal narratives, American. | Actors—
United States—Biography. | Internet personalities—United States—
Biography. | Businesspeople—United States—Biography.
Classification: LCC U53.B47 (ebook) | LCC U53.B47 A3 2019 (print) |
DDC 956.7044/42092 [B]—dc23
LC record available at lccn.loc.gov/2019016176

Printed in the United States of America on acid-free paper

randomhousebooks.com

2 4 6 8 9 7 5 3 1

First Edition

*For my beautiful mother, who has stood by me
through success and failure while I chase my dreams,
despite wishing for a girl when she was pregnant with me.
Don't worry, Mom, there is hope for me yet. Bruce Jenner
didn't transition until he was in his sixties.*

Contents

Thank You for My Service

Chapter 1

Does Anyone Need a Hand?

As an Army Ranger and a ███ contractor, I had the honor
and pleasure of spending some of the best years of my life defending what this country stands for. I did my thing in many different areas of several countries over the better part of a decade. I saw a lot of death. I made a fair share of it myself, dispatching our enemies to the netherworld with extreme prejudice by any means necessary. I wore the uniform with immense pride and deep admiration for those who had worn it long before me, including my father, a Vietnam-era veteran. It was a privilege to be part of a military brotherhood that is second to none.

After leaving the Army following five combat deployments, I never thought I'd be able to replicate the relationships I built within that brotherhood. I assumed that whatever I did next couldn't possibly offer the kind of camaraderie you develop by living and working with the same group of guys, in war zones and on military bases, day in and day out. Over the years, however, I've found ways to compensate for that in my personal life and in my professional life. Early on, if I was missing one of my boys, I'd just hop on a plane and crash on his couch without giving him a chance to warn his wife, like a good friend is supposed to. Later, to stay in touch, I'd start a group text and send a message like "Perfect 10" with a picture of Kim Jong Il's bullet-riddled face taped over the ten ring at my local shooting range, which would inspire them to send range pics of their own, partly to join in the fun and partly to pretend like they're better shooters than me, which is just about as pointless an exercise as arguing on the Internet.

Eventually, though, as I moved on and moved around and some of those older relationships faded into the background, I realized that camaraderie isn't something that only develops between people who've shared the same experience. It's also possible to develop it with new people who share the same values and have had the same *types* of experiences. Guys from the military can work and connect with each other outside the military too. The service is not the only place where you can create bonds with guys who know what it means to sacrifice, to suffer, and to shit in places with no doors on them.

That isn't why I ultimately started a clothing company or a liquor company or joined forces to build a coffee company called Black Rifle Coffee, but it *is* why my partners and I prioritize hiring veterans. We know that they're looking for the same thing in the civilian world that we were: the ability to play with guns, dogs, and explosives while doing some good and keeping our health benefits in the process. Starting a business by veterans, for veterans, is probably the closest I will ever come to re-creating the emotions I felt and the bonds I enjoyed during my time with the Army and the ■■■.

Now if only it could re-create the one thing I have missed more than anything—every waking moment of every day—since I left the military: the thrill of war.

Silently hunting nature's most formidable opponent while implementing years of training to execute a precision raid? Yes, please. High-fiving some jihadi's face into martyrdom with a suppressed AR-15? That's just a warm slice of freedom pie with an ice-cold scoop of America on the side. Understanding the fragile, ephemeral nature of life and then being the one to snatch it away from some fucking terrorist who hates you and wants to kill you and everyone you care about? It's better than Chick-fil-A . . . and let's face it, *nothing is better than Chick-fil-A.*

Yet the most satisfying kind of war story of all, karmically speaking, is when one of these dickless shitbirds suicide-bombs himself into oblivion but fails to take anybody with him because he's fucking stupid. One night, deep in central Iraq on my final deployment, I had the great honor of watching the world's worst terrorist work his special brand of magic.

Our target that night was a set of buildings that either housed or operated as a meeting place for an active cell of insurgents. When that many fighters gather in one place there's usually a bunch of shit worth knowing about them, so our mission was to capture as many of them as we could for intelligence-gathering purposes. We'd been watching these buildings through an ISR (Intelligence, Surveillance, Reconnaissance) drone feed for several hours prior to spinning up from base to confirm that everyone inside was a legitimate fighter, so by the time we got in the air, we knew there was a high probability that they possessed information worth . . . how should I put this . . . extracting? Yeah, the Department of Defense will like that word. I'm going with *extracting*.

The plan was to execute a basic offset infil, which means that the helicopters drop our teams about three to six kilometers from the target location so the enemy can't hear us and we can use the cover of darkness to walk in and fuck their souls in the middle of the night. Everything was going according to plan on our flight into the HLZ (helicopter landing zone) when, wouldn't you know it, the drone feed showed six enemy combatants run out from one of the buildings carrying AK-47s, RPGs, and PKMs (belt-fed machine guns). They jumped into a truck and took off.

In the military we have a name for guys like these—enemy combatants who somehow catch wind of the twenty to twenty-five inbound Americans and choose flight over fight. We call them "squirters" because they are usually holed up inside a juicy soft target where, if you apply enough consistent, vigorous pressure in just the right way, from the front or the rear, eventually something's coming out. The only questions are how much, how fast, and in what direction?

Back at base, our drone operator re-tasked the ISR to chase the squirters as we touched down, jumped out of the helicopter, and started hiking toward the target. About halfway there, we spotted their truck trying to outflank our element. Since they were mobile and we were on foot, our ground force commander immediately cleared an AC-130 gunship to orient to their position and say hello with its 105mm howitzer shells and 40mm Bofors cannons.

A few minutes later, listening to the radio chatter in my capacity as a team leader, two facts soon became clear: (1) the AC-130 had disabled the vehicle, displacing the combatants; and (2) my squad of nine men would reroute to find and handle them while the rest of the platoon headed to the target buildings.

I leaned in to my team.

"Just so you guys know, I guarantee most of them will still be alive when we clear through, so be ready," I instructed. "Load your 40mm, and make sure you're ready to get nasty."

By this point in my service, I had been through enough combat that I didn't fuck around anymore. If I thought there was a credible threat in front of us, we were going in like a Ruth's Chris baked potato—fully loaded—and doming assholes. If I was pieing a hillside and I saw what looked like a dead body lying motionless in the brush, I would put one through its head just to be sure, because half the time the guy wasn't dead at all. When you came up on his position, you'd discover that he was alive and armed, hoping you'd let your guard down. Or, if he was even more patient, he might wait till you got close enough and then blow himself up. After enough of those instances, there was no hesitation or cautious optimism left inside me. If they were known combatants, we made sure they were dead as we tidied up the mess they made.

Once we were all squared away, my squad slowly made its way to the squirters' last known position. Distance-wise it wasn't far, but time-wise you never knew how long it would take. The undulations of the Iraqi desert constantly messed with your depth perception, so when you were looking for something that you didn't have a fixed position on, it almost always caught you by surprise when you finally found it.

Ten minutes in, we saw a flickering glow on the horizon. We'd all seen that glow before. Most of us on the squad had *made* that glow at one time or another. Vehicle fire. The glow guided our way, but we actually ended up hearing the vehicle before we saw it. The heat from the fire was cooking off all the 7.62 AK-47 rounds still in the bed of the truck and the noise was echoing out in all directions.

Following the sound, we crested a berm and finally came upon the burning vehicle. The fire was so powerful that it had completely engulfed the truck and nearly whited out our night vision goggles. It also did that weird thing that fire does where it illuminates everything in the foreground but makes it impossible to see anything behind it. To avoid getting clipped by one of the combatants hiding in the blind spot, we organized our assault in a linear formation. This would also reduce the odds of getting fragged by the truck firing AK rounds in every direction like a drunk Decepticon.

From the ISR footage we knew that there were six of these mangy cats that we had to herd. We found the first three right away, lying on the ground in front of the burning vehicle with their weapons beside them. They were playing dead. Their wounded breathing gave them away. Along with a couple of my squad members, we engaged directly before they could return fire or clack off their suicide vests. Play time was over. America three, Terrorists nil (that's soccer for zero).

As we pushed past the truck, we spotted the fourth man, who had the truck's PKM pointed at me with its 7.62x51mm hundred-round belt ready to rock. How the guy didn't cut me in half with that thing before one of my squad members put two in his head, I'll never know. I got lucky a lot in war. 4–0, America.

That left two more combatants to find. They weren't dead in the vehicle, and they weren't within the typical area of destruction you find after a meet-and-greet with an AC-130 gunship. They could be on foot, stalking us from somewhere beyond the halo of the fire. They could be mortally wounded and no longer a threat. But we didn't know, so we couldn't assume they were neutralized.

Finally clear of the vehicle, I crested another small berm to get a better view of the surrounding area. There were no obvious structures in the immediate vicinity that would have made for a good terrorist hidey-hole, so I knew that the remaining bad guys were probably super close. That's when I saw the top of the head of one of them, no more than twenty meters away, as he presented himself from a prone posture to a kneeling position a little ways down the sloping berm. He was trying to aim his AK-47 up at what I imagined was my silhouette, backlit by the raging inferno behind me. Unfortunately for him, I was locked on and at the high ready with my weapon. I immediately engaged the threat with multiple rounds. (5–0, Good Guys.) As he fell, right behind him the sixth member of the Iraqi Village People finally showed himself. He was unarmed, but he was not empty-handed. Then, just as quickly as he popped up, he disappeared . . . in a large explosion and a blinding cloud of dust.

Remember that scene in *Pulp Fiction* at the beginning of "The Bonnie Situation" when Jules and Vincent are in an apartment to retrieve a stolen case for Marcellus Wallace and they forget to account for the guy who's hiding in the bathroom? Remember when the guy bursts out with a "goddamn hand cannon" and unloads the entire clip at point-blank range and completely misses them? That's exactly what it felt like as we stood there, well within the blast radius of a typical suicide bomber, not just alive but without a scratch on us. Final score: USA 6, Enemy Combatants 0.

Had we seen the vest before it detonated, maybe one of us would have had a spiritual awakening like Jules did, but since it happened before any of us knew what was going on, all we could really do was thank the lord that these assholes had more faith in the Prophet than they had in tactical precision. By blowing himself up against the side of a dirt defilade, at the bottom of it no less, this fucking assclown gave his bomb no room to explode. When our man hit the trigger, most of the shrapnel either blew out the back of his vest, away from us, or out the front, directly into the side of the embankment. Whatever didn't go there sailed harmlessly up over our heads. When the sand settled and the smoke cleared, the only evidence in the immediate vicinity that this guy had even existed was the pothole where he had just been standing and the blood that coated the ground around the hole, like some kind of Salafi spin art.

For someone from the birthplace of mathematics, this guy understood angles for shit. But that's to be expected with a lot of suicide bombers: They're not known for being deep analytical minds who think things through completely. It's hard to get mad at a walking Darwin Award like that, especially when he saves the U.S. government the thirty-three cents it would have cost to shoot him. Still, I managed to find a way, because now he'd made it virtually impossible to identify him.

A lot of people have this Hollywood picture in their heads of war casualties, like one second they're lying there shaking and taking in the enormity of what has happened, then the next moment they accept it, cough up some blood, close their eyes, and die. No, sir. If I just put seven bullets in some dude's head and he didn't see me coming, there's no contemplation, there's just a mess. A mess that I end up having to clean off with the little bit of good drinking water I brought so that our photographer can get a clear(ly useless) picture of the dead combatant. There is no amount of water, no camera angle, no Instagram filter, that is going to make up for the lack of a face. And that is never truer than when you're dealing with a walking IED who is also really bad at terrorism.

On the bright side, we did have most of the other five combatants. We lined them all up by their vehicle, which had burned itself out by this point, and began to catalog and identify them by taking photos and fingerprints. When we turned our attention to Lil' Sammy Suicide Bomber, we discovered to my great displeasure that all we were able to find were his legs and ass. There are three people on this planet I can identify from those body parts alone: Serena Williams, Kim Kardashian, and that South African sprinter who killed his girlfriend. There was no way we were going to get anything useful from the lower half of this dude's body.

Frustrated, I walked away from my squad over to the blast site and started pacing out into the desert on an arc where I thought the blast might have thrown body parts big and sturdy enough to survive the explosion. Maybe I'd get lucky and find a head or some-thing. Fifty meters from the bottom of that little berm, I spotted an arm, severed at the elbow, fingers still attached. Boo-yah. The arm wasn't just important for identifying the final combatant, by the way. It was also the last piece of the puzzle that was going to let us exfil and go the fuck home.

Moments like these are tricky. Those first minutes when the ac-tion feels like it's over and the mission has been completed, that's when the adrenaline dump happens and you're most liable to lose focus or let your emotions take hold of you—whatever they are. Unnoticed and unchecked, a weird anxiety can start to build, and that's when things can go sideways.

As a team leader, it was my job in those situations to stay frosty and read the room, so to speak. If people were too loose, I'd go Scared Straight on them. If they were too amped, I'd bring down the energy. Having just dodged a hail of cooked-off ammo, a dude with a locked-and-loaded PKM, another with an AK, and his peek-a-boo pal the human grenade right behind him, there was a fair amount of nervous tension in the air. There is only one response to a scenario like that: gallows humor.

I grabbed the severed arm by the elbow, trotted back, and just as I got over the berm in full view of the squad, I started waving the hand like I'd just won a beauty pageant.

"Hey, guys!" I shouted. "Does anyone need a hand?!"

The entire squad took a second to register what they were see-ing . . . and finally busted out laughing in a huge wave of catharsis. Once the laughter started, the floodgates opened, as much for me as for them. I'm like a can of Pringles that way: once you pop, I just can't stop.

I held the arm toward the center of my chest and grabbed a fin-ger. "Finally, something I can count on!" Then we arm wrestled. I won. I finished it with a Stone Cold Stunner. To celebrate I threw the hand in the air and waved it around like I just didn't care. Then I curled the fingers into a loose fist. "Who wants the first hand job?" I assured my squad that this was not the bomber's wiping hand, but sadly I had no takers.

It's no wonder Carrot Top had such a long career—you can get a lot out of just one prop.

The poor intel guy tasked with fingerprinting and inputting everything into the computers just glared at me when I held out the arm with the hand fully articulated and tried to input the fingerprints myself one by one. *Boop. Boop. Boop.* "What?" I said, bobbing the arm up and down like a puppet and taking a stab at the voice of a severed limb. "I just want you to run my prints so your friends can go home already!"

When we were all finished, we called in the 160th SOAR (Special Operations Aviation Regiment) to come pick us up. Just for fun, we set their HLZ right next to the pile of dead bodies. Those SOAR dudes are a bunch of hardcore seasoned flyers, but some of their new crew chiefs don't get to see this much death up close. Imagine being the eighteen-year-old aviation crew chief whose job is to man an M240 machine gun on the side of a helicopter and your pilot sets you down next to six dead bodies (ok, five and a half) with giant Sharpie marks labeled 1 through 6, arms and body parts stacked, everything neatly organized into a row.

I looked at the kid and waved as I got on the helicopter. From the look on his face he seemed both awestruck and dumbstruck, so I pulled out my camera to show him the photos we'd just taken. Most of them were for intelligence-gathering and evidentiary purposes. The picture I took of the arm, though, was more of a reminder that this one piece of flesh and bone could have been responsible for five or six more flag-draped metal coffins rolling out of a dull gray C-130 on the tarmac of Dover Air Force Base.

There was nothing especially gruesome about the photos— nothing out of the ordinary—but it was clear from the kid's reaction that he disagreed. After nine or ten of these Ranger glamour shots, he shook his head and turned back to his machine gun. He was intrigued right up until the point when I showed him what real war was like, then he was like, "I'm good." Smart kid.

Looking back, I'm a little disappointed in my behavior in that moment. I completely missed a chance to hold on to the arm a little longer and high-five guys with it as I boarded the helicopter.

Instead I hastily threw it into the pile of dead people to be counted, like a total amateur. In the heat of the moment, though, you can only do what you've been trained to do, and for me that meant making inappropriate jokes to entertain my men (not just myself) and—at least for a minute—help them cut through the horror of war. I mean, what are the chances that the only identifiable part left from a suicide bomber is the arm he detonated his bomb with? How do you let that kind of awesome irony go by without saying something? It's one of those funny little bits of karmic justice that life throws at you so you don't lose your mind.

It's also one of those moments when any sane person has to ask themselves: How the fuck did I get here?

Chapter 2

From Green Day to Green Thumb

Despite being the youngest of six in a military family grow-ing up in Santa Barbara, California, I hadn't put much thought into joining up when I entered high school, largely because I didn't feel like I fit the part. When I looked in the mirror I didn't see a soldier; I saw an awkward, introverted kid, one who loved playing music and who was more interested in science and business than anything else. Instead of playing sports or working on cars or going surfing, like most of the other guys in my class, my extra-curricular interests drew me into two of the coolest groups anyone could ever join on a Southern California high school campus: the botany club and an emo band.

I know what you're thinking: *Bro, those groups must have been total pussy magnets.* And you'd be totally right, broseph, they were. Each one was filled with total pussies. In botany club, all we did was sit around talking about girls and money. The closest we ever got to actual agriculture was bullshitting about how to cross-pollinate the marijuana strains we'd read about in *High Times.* At one point we managed to pull our green thumbs out of our asses long enough to try to build a greenhouse, but that didn't get much past the planning stages.

Things weren't much better in the band, which we called Blind Story, because *of course* we did. I'd gotten taller by the time we actually played some gigs, but I was still way too skinny, my teeth were a little too bucked for my mouth—I basically looked like a Christmas nutcracker—and if my jet-black Flock of Seagulls haircut wasn't quite repellent enough, I decided to play bass, just to make sure all the girls knew that the last vagina I'd been inside of was the one I'd come out of.

There's nothing particularly unique about that combination of physical characteristics or even my circumstances, but when you throw in the strong military pedigree—and the fact that things only got more awkward as I grew from adolescent boy to pubescent teenager—what you ended up with was not G.I. Joe but "Gee, I don't think you're ever going to have sex."

Don't misunderstand: I don't regret a single second I spent in Blind Story or in botany club. Surprisingly, when you're not fucking, you can actually learn stuff. In the band, I got experience with teamwork and finding my place as part of a larger unit. In botany club, I learned one of the most important lessons of all: how to hustle.

When we first tried to build that greenhouse, the school made us pay for our own supplies, so we needed to generate cash. The cheerleaders had the car wash. The marching band had the bake sale. The swim team had rich parents. We needed to find our own thing. Besides being complete cock pockets, the only marketable skill any of us had was my ability to grill hamburgers like a boss. So that's what we did. Every day at lunchtime, I got behind an old Weber grill and we slung burgers in the courtyard like Avon Barksdale slinging crack in the low-rises. It wasn't long before business was booming. All the kids were fiending for our shit. We were selling out regularly and making some decent coin, at least for high school kids.

As the burger business grew and grew, one of the vice principals finally asked me if we had authorization. I didn't lie, but I also didn't answer her question: I told her we were raising money for the botany club. She let it slide for a while, but eventually, the school realized they were losing lunch money to our little operation, and they shut us down. That's what happens when a scrappy upstart with a better product carves out a niche for itself in a market previously dominated by a natural monopoly. They snuff it out. All these lessons would help me immensely when I started getting into for-real business a decade later, but in the moment it made me hate everything school-related.

It wasn't until the second half of high school that the military started to have some appeal for me. It began when two of my older brothers, Alan and Davis, were preparing to graduate from Marine Corps boot camp together and my parents and I went down to Camp Pendleton to visit them for Family Day.

Family Day is supposed to be an awesome day—a celebration. Except for the last day of school, there aren't many days that a fifteen-year-old kid looks forward to like, "Holy shit, I can't wait for that day to come." But when you grow up with a hardcore veteran as a father, and your older brothers, who are like heroes to you, are graduating from boot camp together, it is a big fucking deal. And it is no joke.

I'll never forget that Family Day. It was September 11, 2001.

The culminating event of boot camp takes place two weeks prior to graduation. It's a fifty-four-hour suckfest called "The Crucible" that, like the play of the same name by Arthur Miller, is excruciating to get through if you're not a total masochist. But the Crucible is a mandatory experience if you want to call yourself a Marine. It's a never-ending parade of marching, obstacle course running, team-building, and other sweet mental challenges designed to test your endurance and your sanity, all on very little sleep and even less food.

Davis got through the Crucible without much problem—just the normal bumps and bruises, aches and pains. Alan, on the other hand, struggled quite a bit, which was not like him. It took everything he had, plus a little more, to get through the two-and-a-half-day ordeal. The middle brother, Alan was the real badass of the Best family. He was the guy who never got tired, who encouraged everyone else to push through. If he had that much of a problem, something had to be wrong with him. It turns out, Alan had been sick for the last month of boot camp, coughing and spitting up blood. At one point he even had a 106-degree fever that caused him to lose his vision for three days. That's fine if you're one of these low-rent jihadis whose training involves shooting blind over walls and around corners, but in the U.S. military we like to see what we're doing, so Alan went to the infirmary to get checked out. They did some chest X-rays and diagnosed him almost immediately with full-blown pneumonia.

Well, no wonder he struggled! His lungs were suffocating him from the inside out. Hillary Clinton couldn't make it to her car with pneumonia; I can't imagine anyone finishing the Crucible with a bad case of it, let alone the last week of boot camp and the physical and mental beatdown still left to endure. But try raising your hand and telling your drill sergeant you don't feel well. See how that goes.

"Why don't you keep your fucking skirt down, Marilyn, and if you need a good cry, rent the fucking Notebook! *Get the fuck back in formation!"*

A few days later, we got a call at home from the Navy doctor who had examined Alan. Pneumonia wasn't the only thing he was suffering from. A biopsy conducted during the same exam found a "calcium deposit" in his neck that led to a much more serious diagnosis: Stage 2 Hodgkin's lymphoma. For those of you who are not familiar with this wonderfully destructive disease, Hodgkin's is a cancer of the lymphatic system that requires radiation and chemotherapy. It's not one of the more fatal cancers, thank God, but it still sucks a mountain of ass. In some of the most superfun cases, it requires stem cell transplants over a twelve- to eighteen-month period to knock it out.

The night before heading down to Camp Pendleton for Family Day, my parents spent the entire evening talking about how they were going to break the news to Alan. I politely suggested a Male Stripper–gram because, I told them, that wasn't the only calcium deposit Alan had been hiding, if you catch my drift. They did not appreciate my brotherly joking and kicked me out of the kitchen while they tried to navigate the situation. This was their child, on the doorstep of achieving a lifelong dream, and they were going to be the ones who might have to take it all away.

Then things got even more fucked. The next morning—Tuesday, September 11—I was abruptly woken up for school by my mother yelling, "Get in the bathroom, now!" She had an old-style TV hooked up next to her vanity where she did her morning makeup. The first plane had already hit the North Tower. While I stood there confused, in total disbelief like the rest of the country, the second plane struck the South Tower.

During the four-hour drive to Camp Pendleton in our shitty brown Buick sedan, we had the radio on in search of new details and updates as the situation unfolded in real time. News reports were full of endless speculation the entire trip down. All I could think to myself was "I hope the Marine base isn't a target for these assholes." My father, for his part, simply stared straight ahead out at the road, exhaling deeply every so often. Nothing more. He didn't say a word, which meant nobody else said anything either. In those first twenty-four hours, nobody knew what the fuck was going on, but my dad knew: Two of his sons were about to go to war. Well, one of them, anyway.

When we arrived at Camp Pendleton, the place was a total shit show, and we quickly learned that graduation ceremonies were postponed indefinitely due to the base-wide lockdown. There were obviously more important things going on, which we totally understood. None of that changed the fact that we still had to tell Alan about his diagnosis. You can't imagine how much it sucks to have to tell your brother and one of your heroes, on one of the most important days in American history, that he had Hodgkin's lymphoma:

> **Me:** Congrats on being a Marine, bro.
> **Alan:** Thanks, Mat.
> **Me:** By the way, you have cancer. You better semper fi-nd a doctor.

Thankfully, I wasn't the one who had to break it to him. My dad pulled him aside and told him privately. Alan was pretty stoic about it, which was to be expected. What I didn't expect was that the ramifications of my dad's news had completely changed in the time it had taken us to drive to Pendleton. When those nineteen martyrdom-loving motherfuckers flew four planes into three buildings and a field in Pennsylvania, Alan's issues were no longer just about overcoming cancer. They now included the suddenly urgent question of whether or not he'd be able to deploy with his unit and fight for his country. And if Davis got deployed without Alan—because he was in the middle of a chemo cycle or a radiation regimen—that would have been what we Best brothers like to call a real kick in the dick.

We hung around Pendleton for a couple days until finally they conducted the graduation ceremonies on the fourteenth. This was now obviously different from any other boot camp graduation in years or even decades, maybe ever. As I looked around, I could see the tension on the parents' faces, knowing that their kids were more than likely going to war. It was such a stark contrast with the young Marines who were graduating. Their expressions signaled some anxiety, of course, but also their excitement. You could tell they couldn't wait to get the fuck out of there, go to SOI (School of Infantry), and then deploy as fast as they could to blow these motherfuckers off the planet. I'll never forget that look on their faces. It seared itself into my memory. It was actually a big part of the shift that was beginning to take place in my head—from emo dork to future soldier.

That afternoon, after commencement ended and my brothers said their goodbyes to their friends, we all piled back into the car for the drive back to Santa Barbara. *All of us*. My brothers in the window seats, me sitting bitch. There wasn't much talking. It was just like the drive down a few days earlier, except now the radio wasn't spewing speculation and panic. It was painting a picture of a villain most of us had never heard of: Al-Qaeda.

———

In the days and months following Alan's return to Santa Barbara, do you want to guess what he did? I'll tell you what he didn't do: He didn't fucking complain. Alan tackled cancer the way he approached everything in life—head on. He followed the protocols, he ate as much as he could, and he tried to stay in shape. I would see him come back from chemo looking pale and green but still in high spirits. We would be watching TV together, and he would quietly get up, throw up in the bathroom, and come back as if nothing had happened. He treated treatment like a duty, and as a reward, we treated him like nothing had changed. Translation: We fucked with him *constantly*.

There were a lot of "Hey, Alan, can you stand next to the microwave and heat this up for me? You have cancer already, so what's the difference?" If we picked him up from the hospital, we'd take back roads and tell him that we were looking out for him by avoiding cellular towers. I'm not sure how much he enjoyed it at the time, but I know he appreciated it when he got older, because he understood, just like I eventually would, that having a fucked-up sense of humor is probably as important to keeping a soldier alive as his weapons or his armor.

In March of 2002, seven months after Alan's diagnosis, the doctor declared him cancer-free. Six weeks after finishing treatment, with only thin patches of hair having grown back, he went to SOI. The doctors told him it would be two years before he would be considered full duty and deployable. Alan had a few things to tell them, too.

By a roll of the dice, my brothers' unit hadn't gotten the call to deploy to Afghanistan in the first months of fighting after 9/11. But in early 2003, eighteen months after their graduation, they were told that they were headed to Kuwait for the pre-stage of the invasion of Iraq. By this time Alan had been cancer-free for eleven months. The problem was, the military required you to be free and clear for twelve months in order to deploy, plus the notes on all his charts indicated that they thought he would need an extra year of recovery. So close, and at the same time so far.

Did Alan complain? C'mon, I think you know the answer to that by now. He handled his fucking business. The first thing he did was go through the standard military process, filling out paperwork, getting signatures, getting approvals to try and become deployable. Of course, since this was the military, things took forever, and it wasn't until the day before his and Davis's company was slated to leave that he found out it had gotten all dicked up and he had been denied. When he got the news, he tried another tack, making an appointment for a pre-deployment physical the next day to try to secure clearance through medical channels before his company's plane took off from Pendleton Airfield.

"Sir, I gotta be with my platoon when they deploy today," he told the military doctor.

The doctor nodded, seeing the eagerness in Alan's eyes. "All right. Stand up, let's have a look at you."

As the doctor ran his exam, Alan passed everything. Then came the standard check of the lymph nodes, which is a dead giveaway for Hodgkin's patients, even ones whose cancer is in remission. The doctor put both hands on Alan's neck, lightly pressed on the lymph nodes, and promptly stopped the exam.

"How do your lymph nodes feel? Swollen? Sore?"

"Not at all. They feel good. I feel great."

"Uh-huh. Because to me they feel swollen," the doctor said in a serious tone.

"Well, I'm not sure what you mean. Like I said, I feel great. I was around a couple fellows who were smoking cigarettes last night, though. Maybe their secondhand smoke briefly polluted my lungs—"

"Son, that shit isn't going to fly. You're a recovering cancer patient, and your lymph nodes are swollen. I'm afraid I can't medically clear you to deploy. I'm sorry."

"But I've been done with chemo for eleven months—"

"It's for your own good. I'm sure you'll be fine for the next deployment."

"Yeah, but my unit is leaving tonight." Alan was persistent.

"My hands are tied. Sorry, son. Don't worry, the war isn't going anywhere." He patted Alan on the shoulder with the maximum allowable amount of sympathy for an E-3 at the bottom of the Marine Corps food chain. Which is to say, none. The doctor walked out, leaving Alan momentarily dejected, then pissed. This was an "official" military determination that would get reported to his unit commander, which meant there was no way to get his name on that activation order or his ass on that plane.

For the ordinary person, this would have been the ballgame. But Alan isn't ordinary. He is a master bullshit artist. He is the fucking Michelangelo of feces painting. In the parking lot outside the medical building, he called the civilian oncologist who had cleared him for SOI eleven months earlier. Alan explained the situation—well, *a* situation: He was about to leave on a "training exercise" that was only going to be "three weeks" as part of a "temporary deployment" to a place that was absolutely 100 percent *not* in a war zone, and he needed to get a physical because his military doctors wanted a second opinion in order to clear him. It made sense to the oncologist, as all good lies do to all people, and he agreed to see Alan that afternoon.

Alan's oncologist was an hour and a half away and, with no military affiliation, had no clue what was going on or what was at stake. So when Alan got there, he nonchalantly walked into the exam room and made it seem like this was the most run-of-the-mill, check-the-box, stamp-the-passport visit in the world. Which it was—until he felt Alan's lymph nodes.

"These seem swollen, Alan."

Here's the thing about civilian doctors who practice around the edges of a military population: They may be *adjacent* to our world, but that's a lot different than being in it, and the truth is, they know fuck-all about how the military actually operates. So when a young, healthy-looking Marine walks into one of their exam rooms ramrod straight, confident, and unflappable, then lies right to their fucking face, they have no incentive to dig deeper and no clue that they're getting ridden hard and put away wet. Plus, Alan had already done this to the doctor a year earlier, when he fed the doctor the line of bullshit that got him cleared for SOI before he should have been. This guy was used to the feel of the man in the saddle taking him for a ride.

"Oh, I know, but I'm obviously fine," Alan said. "I mean, you declared me cancer-free eleven months ago, and truthfully this is just a formality the military requires so they can cover their own asses. Also, I'll be home in three weeks. It's almost like a retreat in a way. It's not like I'm invading Iraq or anything."

That was enough for Hall of Fame Hippocrates, apparently, because he signed off and sent my brother on his way.

When Alan got back to base, there were still a few "small" hurdles he needed to overcome. First, he needed a ride to Kuwait, because his company, Echo, had just left, including our brother Davis. There were other companies still scurrying around preparing to deploy the next day, and the day after that, and the day after that . . . but *his* company was already flying the friendly skies. So he hatched a plan to go standby with Fox Company, which was leaving the next day.

It was a solid plan, except for the next problem: Since he wasn't officially cleared to deploy, he didn't have any equipment. No helmet, no body armor, no nothing. It's one thing to talk your way onto another company's plane; it's another thing entirely to come up with a plausible reason why you have no gear. So Alan didn't even try. Instead, as he told me later, he "found some loose equipment laying on the floor by the lockers" of other companies who weren't about to deploy. Then he added, "Some of the lockers might have been open, it was hectic around there." You know what else is hectic, Alan? The tornado of bullshit whipping around your head.

The rest of the night and into the next day, Alan scrambled like a man on fire to get onto Fox's plane. Once he got approval and was safely onboard, he triumphantly grabbed a seat and took a breath for the first time in seventy-two hours. He looked around at everyone to see if they were as excited as he was. That's when he realized his next and biggest problem: All these dudes had guns. He did not. Whoopsies! How the hell was he going to get a weapon? Oh well, one hustle at a time.

When the flight landed, Alan caught a lift to base with Fox Company. When he got off the truck and took his first official step onto a U.S. military base in wartime conditions, a guy from Alpha Company saw him and stopped him in his tracks.

"Best?" he said in disbelief. "What the fuck are you doing here?"

"Oh, I hitched a ride."

"Dude, Davis is going to fucking shit his pants. Does he know?"

"What do you think?"

The Alpha Company guy laughed and disappeared, but Alan had other things on his mind. Big, long, hard, black things that gave him immense pleasure to wrap his hands around. Also, he needed a gun. How does one go about getting a firearm in a war zone when you're not even supposed to be there in the first place? Turns out, you just ask. Alan showed up to his unit HQ, talked to the first sergeant of another company, and asked to sign out a gun. Simple as that. No one even said anything to him, and he went along as if it was business as usual.

Within twenty minutes of Alan being there, word had reached Davis, who immediately bolted out to see if the rumors were true.

"Bro, what the fuck are you doing here?" Davis asked.

"Turns out Southwest flies *really* far east now."

Davis had so many questions. Alan patiently answered them all, the way you do when you're explaining something awesome you've done and you're just waiting for the other person to catch up and agree with you. Davis just shook his head. None of the answers made any logical sense; they were only understandable if you knew Alan as well as Davis does. Ultimately, the "how" of it all didn't matter. It was the "why" that was important, and Davis was glad that Alan wasn't missing out, because not being over there with the guys really would have killed him. Well, that and the cancer.

I didn't even find out about Alan's little stunt until about a week later. I was chilling at home when the phone rang. When I answered, I heard the crackling of what I now recognize as a SAT (satellite) phone, followed by a faint voice.

"Hey man, what's up?" he said, as if he didn't have a care in the world.

"Hello? Alan, is that you?"

"Yeah man, I'm in Kuwait."

"What?" I said, stunned.

"Yeah, I can't really talk. I only have a minute on this thing. Tell everyone that I love them and that I'm here with Davis and it's all good."

"Okay. You guys kick some ass. Love you guys."

"Same here."

The phone call ended as quickly as it had started. Knowing what I know now, I have no idea how the fuck a lowly E-3 in the Marine Corps even got to use a SAT phone. Back then, they were like a hundred dollars per minute. When my dad got home and I told him Alan had called, and where he'd called from, and *how* he'd called, my dad just shook his head, just like Davis had.

But that was Alan: unstoppable. There was no obstacle he couldn't overcome, no bull he couldn't shit. Not cancer, and certainly not the pesky regulations of the United States military. He never complained, he never made excuses, and he never asked for pity or a break. He just did his job. That, as much as anything else, really pushed the baby out of the stroller for me when it came to the idea of joining the military.

Alan's calmness and deliberation and fortitude were an inspiration for me from the day he got the news—of his diagnosis, of the planes hitting the building, of the long road ahead for him. I was fired up for patriotic reasons too, of course: I wanted to do everything I could to defend my country and the freedom it provides to all of us. But the real motivation came from within my own family. Watching how Alan and Davis turned into men as the war filled them with purpose, I remember thinking, "I want *that*."

Chapter 3

You're in the Army, *Now*?!

There is a simple truth that comes with sibling rivalry, especially when you're the baby of the family: It is never as easy as following in your brothers' footsteps. Doing what they have done is never enough. You have to exceed them. To quote Jay-Z, "You have to go farther, go further, go harder, and if not, then why bother?" If they learn to skydive, you have to BASE jump. If they BASE jump, you have to HALO jump. If they HALO jump, I don't know, then fucking Red Bull it from space. It doesn't matter. The point is: In my mind, I had to be better than my brothers.

This quest to be the better Best started with learning everything I could about the military. I immersed myself in military culture and quickly became obsessed to a nearly unhealthy degree, like the Japanese are with poop or the Germans are . . . well, also with poop. I started with movies. I watched every single war movie I could get my hands on: *Platoon, Full Metal Jacket, Born on the Fourth of July, The Deer Hunter, Patton, The Thin Red Line, Black Hawk Down, Hamburger Hill, Saving Private Ryan, Apocalypse Now, Major Payne*. I studied these war flicks the way conspiracy theorists study the Zapruder film—pantsless.

After I was done with every military film ever made, I turned my attention to learning about generals. George Washington, Ulysses S. Grant, Dwight D. Eisenhower. We mostly remember them as presidents now, but as generals those motherfuckers iced a serious number of bad guys in the name of #Merica. And as much as I eventually wanted to be the guy who put the bullets in those bad guys, initially I wanted to understand strategy and the psyche of the war mind as well. I wanted to understand what it meant to be *lethal* in every way possible.

Next I tried to memorize all the different ranks in all branches of the military. I still wasn't sure at this point where I wanted to enlist after high school, but wherever I ended up I was sure there would be men and women there who were not only bigger, meaner, faster, smarter, and stronger than me, they would also be in charge. I was confident that I would be able to recognize the hellfire headed my way from the looks on their faces, but why not get better at being able to identify it by the rank on their shoulders? Stars, bars, stripes, and oak leaf clusters—those were the symbols of the people who could fuck my world up.

Sooner or later, I would have to choose a branch. The easy route would have been to join the Marines. My dad was a Marine, my brothers were Marines, I had a general feel for how things worked over there—it would have made sense. But how could I be better than them if all I did was do the same thing they did? You know what they say: If you want to be the best Best, you have to beat the best Bests. (People do say that, I swear.)

Based on my intensive research of war movies, the surest way to outshine my brothers was to forgo basic infantry and join Special Operations. Historically, Marine infantry was "the tip of the spear," but for a few decades now it's been Special Operations who have been the cutting edge. Unfortunately, the Marines didn't really offer a good path toward that goal when I was ready to enlist in 2004. The branch with the most options was the Army. They had ███████████, the Green Berets, the Rangers and—with the exception of *Full Metal Jacket*—they also had the best movies.

As the Army path came into focus, my determination to enlist became fully consuming, and all the other stuff I was doing to pass the time in high school started to fade away. *Bye-bye, Botany Club. It's been real, Blind Story.* I started hanging out with guys who seemed to be on a similar trajectory, and I spent my down time trying to figure out the best way to prepare for boot camp and get into Special Operations. I knew that the Rangers required, at a minimum, scoring an 11x Option 40 contract to fast-track to the unit.

A few definitions are in order here. "11" is the MOS (military occupational specialty) designation for infantry, which is just military jargon for "the dudes who get to kill bad guys." The "x" is the general infantry designation, which means that you aren't pigeon-holed into a certain method of shooting them. The "Option 40" part is what gets you the slot in RASP (Ranger Assessment and Selection Program), which gives you the chance to sneak up on these bad guys and shoot them right in the fucking face in the dead of the night. Pew personified. The question I had was "How do I get me one of those?"

In retrospect, I should have bitten the bullet and asked my dad or my brothers what to do. But in the same way that the youngest always has to exceed the eldest, the youngest can't show any vulnerability. I couldn't seem weak or uncertain to those jackals or they would have eaten me alive:

> **Mat:** Hey guys, what should I do to prepare for Army Rangers?
> **Alan:** Don't ever quit.
> **Davis:** Actually you *should* quit . . . being such a pussy.
> **Mat:** Dad?
> **Dad:** I can't hear the game over your feelings.

Instead, I approached a kid named Travis, who was a senior when I was a junior and had expressed interest in enlisting after high school.

"Hey man, you still thinking about joining the military?" I asked.

"Hell yeah, man. That's all I think about every day," he replied.

"Cool, me too. What do you think about ROTC? That seems like something we should get into. My brothers were in—"

"No dude, that's useless," Travis shot back. "We need to get into something *harder*. Something to get us even more prepared."

"Shit. What will get us more prepared than ROTC?" I asked.

Travis turned and looked around, all conspiratorial-like, making sure no one was listening.

"Civil Air Patrol," he said, squinting and nodding, like he actually knew what the fuck he was talking about. I didn't really know anything about ROTC or Civil Air Patrol at the time, so I had no way of judging them against each other, but I didn't feel like I needed to, because the conviction in Travis's eyes had already sold me.

"I'm in."

The next day, Travis and I enrolled in the after-school program known as Civil Air Patrol. In case you are as unfamiliar with Civil Air Patrol as I was when I signed up, let me sum it up for you: The only difference between a member of the Civil Air Patrol and a Webelo Scout is pubic hair. Even our uniforms were more ridiculous than what the Webelos had. The Webelos might look like a Little League team made up of park rangers, but at least their uniforms fit properly and looked like actual uniforms. Civil Air Patrol uniforms were baggy pieces of shit that looked like pre-packaged Army costumes from one of those inflatable roadside Halloween stores shaped like a giant pumpkin.

Putting on that uniform and leaving the house during daylight hours ended up being the hardest part of Civil Air Patrol. Occasionally, we'd do these weird drills like lying on our backs and holding a two-by-four over our heads for five minutes straight. To this day I don't know what the purpose of that drill was: Simulate an Amish barn raising in zero g? Your guess is as good as mine. I remember one afternoon the instructor trying to get stern with us and saying, "Can you fellows give me twenty push-ups?" As a kid who wanted to be the tip of the spear, I was starting to feel distinctly like the shaft.

If that wasn't bad enough, the rest of my time in Civil Air Patrol was dedicated to standing around and listening to guys talk about planes the same way they talked about girls: fantasizing about them from a distance, obsessing over every little detail, arguing about which ones were the sexiest, and hoping one day they'd actually get to go up inside of one.

While some people are able to find a positive path through programs like Civil Air Patrol, after a month I knew it wasn't for me. I'm more of a "roll up your sleeves and get dirty" kind of guy. Dressing up in a costume and learning the names of military things out of a book was never going to fulfill my desire to serve. So I bailed.

I didn't even bother trying to join ROTC after that. I was done playing make-believe. Instead, I just started running as much as I could and doing push-ups and sit-ups every day. The hardest part was the waiting. Technically, I couldn't enlist until I turned seventeen, and even then it wasn't going to be easy. You can't just walk into a recruiter's office, slap your driver's license down on the desk like you're checking out bowling shoes, and announce: "My name is Mat Best, and I want to kill people for America!" As a minor, you need *both* your parents' signatures on documents that basically say, "We recognize, as our son's legal guardians, that by signing this piece of paper we are saying that we're okay with him stepping in front of bullets." I had a hard time getting my parents to sign field trip permission slips, they were so protective of me. I had no idea how many hoops I might have to jump through to get their John and Jane Hancocks on these enlistment papers.

When asking for something this big—whether it's enlistment papers, your first gun, or asking your girlfriend to have a threesome for the first time—you always start with the toughest nut to crack. In this situation, I thought for sure that would be my mom. If she said yes, the likelihood my dad would also say yes pretty much doubled. If she tried to defer—"Well, what does your father say?"—then I'd be able to concentrate all my conniving teenage energy on a single target. And to be honest, I wasn't too worried about my dad's response. I figured the only thing he might ask was, "It's not the fucking Coast Guard, is it?"

The day I got the paperwork, I brought it home and spent all night in my room rehearsing how I was going to sell it to my mom. I prepared a whole speech that appealed to her sense of fairness ("Come on, Ma, you let my brothers do it! Why can't I go and try not to get killed!"), that had just the right amount of baby-boy begging in it, and that ever so subtly preyed on her patriotism ("America is under attack, Mom! WTF?").

The whole thing was a delicate dance that I could very easily fuck up if I wasn't careful. Moms are like good teachers: They are hard graders and have well-honed bullshit detectors. You can *try* to tell them that the dog ate your homework, and they'll give you the benefit of the doubt, but then they'll ask you what kind of dog you have, and what her name is, and how long you've had her. And when you don't have answers to those questions, that's when they'll send you to detention and tell you that they've secretly always loved the other kids more than you.

Nope, no trust issues here. You can totally have my six-digit iPhone lock screen passcode.

The next morning when I went downstairs for breakfast, I took a deep breath and worked up the courage to pitch my mom as she was washing dishes.

"Mom, I want to enlist in the military."

"When?" she said.

"Right now."

"But you're only seventeen!"

"I know. That's why I need you to sign these documents."

My heart stopped as she put the dishes down and turned to look at me. Mentally, I started to chamber my speech. Emotionally, I worked to steady my trigger finger, because you only get one shot at unloading a magazine of hollow-pointed sympathy bullets into your mother. After a few seconds, she looked down and shook her head. *Here it comes*, I thought.

"Okay. If this is what you are passionate about, you—"

"You let my brothers do it!" I shouted back, not actually hearing a word she was saying.

"—can go too."

Well, shit.

I was totally unprepared for her to be so cool about this, though in retrospect I shouldn't have been. My mom was the only woman in a house with six boys. She kept that house together, figuratively and sometimes quite literally. She was Captain Calm of the U.S.S. *Clusterfuck*. Plus, she was no fool. She looked at the world with clearer eyes than any of us did. Think about it: She married a military man in a military family. She raised a bunch of boys intent on following in those footsteps, boys who trained to run *toward* the people shooting at them and who, in that training, taught themselves to feel invincible. She was the one thousands of miles away with the very real understanding that possibly more than one of the people she loves most in this world might not come home. It takes a special kind of person to live that life and not let the uncertainty and the fear affect everyone around you. You need to be strong, you need to be resilient, you need to be a patriot, and it doesn't hurt if you can make chocolate chip cookies with just the right amount of gooeyness in the middle when your kid is not feeling well. My mom was all of those things, in spades. And culottes.

There should be a congressional medal for moms like her, though at the time the first emotion that washed over me was actually disappointment. I'd crafted this ingenious, unimpeachable argument in defense of my plan, and now I didn't even get to use it. She'd stolen my thunder by being awesome, thanks a lot, Mom. *Keep your shit together,* I thought. *Keep that speech holstered.* Little did I know, this was only the first of many times when I would have to work hard to accept someone's unconditional surrender to my demands instead of getting to blow them away like I *really* wanted.

Still a little off balance, I figured I should seize the moment and go straight to my dad to lock this fucker down. Since he's a proud veteran, I thought getting his sign-off would be an easy task, especially with my mom already onboard. He'd understand, sign right away, I'd go in for the hug, instead he'd give me the handshake, I'd grow up that day, and then we'd cut to a commercial for Cialis and reverse mortgages.

Man, was I wrong.

When I handed him the paperwork, he looked at it, gave me a stern look, then told me to sit down.

I knew what that meant. My mom understood the passion aspect of military service. She didn't just want her boys to be all they could be; she wanted them to be happy and fulfilled too. My dad could give a fuck about my passion if it didn't also have some purpose behind it. He'd served, he knew what war is, he knew what it *really* meant. He wanted to make sure I knew what it meant as well. He wanted to know that I understood what I was getting myself into.

"You know we are at war, right?"

"Yes, sir," I replied.

"You know this isn't going to end anytime soon, right?"

"Maybe when I get there I can help speed up the process."

"Uh-huh. Yeah, war is pretty quick, it will probably be over the day after you get there."

"Well, I didn't mean—"

"Let me tell you something about war, Mat. It's a bitch. And you have no control over it. You're going to be doing things that you'll hate, that you'll find pointless, and there will be rules and decisions you'll have to follow that you won't understand. You'll have a lot of questions that will go unanswered. There's going to be a lot of assholes who think they know what they are doing. They will be wrong, and you will have to do it anyway. You understand?"

"Yes, sir, I do."

I mean, how could I not say that? Pointless tasks and stupid rules? Unanswered questions? Know-it-all assholes? No say over anything? He was basically describing what it's like to grow up as the youngest in a military household. I'd taken more than my fair share of bites out of that shit sandwich. Even if I hadn't, this was my dream. It felt like my true calling. I was going to tell my old man whatever I thought he wanted to hear.

My dad shook his head, knowing full well that I didn't have a fucking clue. But as he looked at me nervously trying to sit up straight in my chair at the kitchen table across from him, he could see that it wasn't doe-eyed passion that was in my eyes. It was determination. So he did what any good father would do. He chose to believe in me and signed the papers.

"I love you. Don't get yourself killed."

"I won't, Dad."

"I'm going to hold you to that," he said, and then he walked out of the house, got in his car, went to work, and we never spoke about it again.

Chapter 4

Baby, It's Cold Outside,
So Please Piss on Me

The path to a Ranger Battalion begins the same way for every infantryman with an 11x Option 40 contract: fifteen weeks at One-Station Unit Training (OSUT), then three weeks at Airborne School, then four weeks at RASP. All of which takes place in and around Fort Benning, outside Columbus, Georgia.

Let me tell you, I have been lucky in my career(s) to travel all over the world. I've met some awesome people and seen some amazingly beautiful places. But I've also been to some real shitholes, and Columbus, Georgia is the shittiest shithole of them all. If its motto isn't "Spread the butt cheeks of Dixie and follow the smell," someone needs to start a petition. How else do you describe a river town on the Alabama border whose crown jewels are three Waffle House franchises within a half-mile of each other?

For infantry, OSUT is ten weeks of basic training and five weeks of advanced individual training, all in one place. The Army says that they combined the two phases to increase unit camaraderie, which it does, but there are other good reasons to keep a bunch of jacked-up eighteen- and nineteen-year-olds penned in for as long as you can when you're training them to be badass killers. After ten weeks of total isolation around a bunch of other dudes, can you imagine putting us on a plane to some other base? No airport bartender or female flight attendant would be safe:

Flight Attendant: Thank you for your service.
Infantryman: It would be my honor to service you.

OSUT sucks in the same boring way that the basic training of every other branch of the military sucks. You do the push-ups, march the miles, eat the shit, do the drills, blah blah blah—I'm up, he sees me, moving on.

Airborne School *sounds* cool, but really all you have to do to get through it is run five miles in less than forty minutes and then jump out of a plane five times without breaking your leg or dying. The running part is pretty easy if you're in decent shape. One time I broke a shoelace three miles into an afternoon run, and instead of stopping to re-rig the shoelace in the eyelets and re-secure the boot, I threw the boot into the woods like an idiot and Forrest Gumped it the last two miles, well within the allotted time. Don't get me wrong, I'm proud of having gone through Airborne, but for someone who has signed up to be a professional face shooter and had volunteered to run at bullets for $25,000 a year, the physical aspects of the school aren't especially difficult.

Proving to yourself that you have the balls to jump out of a perfectly good airplane is where the real test in Airborne is, particularly once you realize that the whole jump procedure is "streamlined" for efficiency's sake. You have to trust someone else to pack your chute, for example. And not just anyone—someone who has *also* agreed to run at bullets for minimum wage. Then, unlike traditional skydiving, you don't have full control over your risers (those sweet little toggles that control the steering of your parachute), which means they're pretty much just fallers. This makes sense when you consider that, in a war zone, you'd like to land as soon as possible. But in training, during a "mass exit" at altitude, what ends up happening is that you play three-dimensional Frogger with twenty-five other jumpers.

One day the winds were gusting like Zeus farts and all I could do to get through being thrown uncontrollably through the air during my jump was to sing the chorus to "Dust in the Wind." I truly felt in that moment that I had no control over my life or death. It was in the hands of '70s supergroup Kansas . . . or possibly fate.

I survived, but others were not so lucky. Throughout my time in the military, I've seen a few Rangers die or get medically retired from injuries sustained during jumps and training exercises. During jump week in the class before mine, a female soldier's parachute suffered a major malfunction and she burned in, unfortunately losing her life from her injuries. About a year later, a fellow Ranger fell to his death during an airfield seizure exercise. Another parachutist got blown right under his canopy and stole the air that was keeping him aloft. Suffice to say, dropping to the ground with no lift isn't pretty. Our awareness of these kinds of deaths didn't make our own jump week harder *per se*, but they were very real reminders that everything we were doing had life-or-death consequences, even in training.

Around that time, two weeks into Airborne, I got a call from my cousin who was a full-bird colonel and who used to be a platoon leader in Ranger Battalion. He was an absolute legend in my mind, and a call from him was a big fucking deal to me. My mother had kept in contact with him throughout my training and had let him know that I would soon be going through RASP if I passed (a.k.a. "did not fall to my death in") Airborne School. He knew from his own experience that not everyone is meant to jump out of an airplane, and I think he was checking in to see whether I was one of those guys.

"How is it going so far?" he asked.

"Easy breezy."

"Sure," he said, knowing full well that I'd just spent the last four months getting my shit pushed in. "I hear you're going to RASP after you graduate."

RASP is the final step that determines whether or not you have what it takes to join one of the three battalions of the 75th Ranger

Regiment. The three are 1st Battalion at Hunter Army Airfield in Savannah, Georgia; 2nd Battalion at Fort Lewis in Tacoma, Washington; and 3rd Battalion right here at luxurious Fort Benning in Columbus, Georgia.

"Where do you want to go after RASP?" he asked.

"I really want to go to Fort Lewis, 2/75, but I'm not sure if that will happen."

"You never know," my cousin said. "Keep your chin up and good luck."

I wanted Fort Lewis for two reasons: I wanted to head back west to be closer to my family down in Santa Barbara, and during this time of the war, the Ranger battalions were on cycled deployments, and the 2/75 had just been pushed forward. This meant that if I got 2nd Battalion, I'd be able to deploy immediately instead of having to cool my heels for several months like the dudes in 1st or 3rd Battalion.

Regardless of how I performed at RASP, I had no idea where I'd wind up, because the military does not have a reputation for granting the wishes of its newest recruits. If you wanted to go to the 1/75, you'd end up at 2nd Battalion. If you wanted to go to the 2/75, you'd end up at 1st Battalion. If you wanted the 3/75 . . . well, you'd end up at the 3/75, because 3rd Battalion is in Columbus, Georgia, and as I've said, nothing sucks more than Columbus.

It's only fitting that RASP also calls Columbus home, because this is when shit starts to get real and the suckfest kicks into high gear. The day after Airborne ended, three Ranger instructors happily met our graduating class to shuttle us to their compound and start the selection process. By "shuttle" I of course mean that they made us run—with all of our gear, personal effects, and duffel bags—the couple of miles up the road. And by "selection process" I mean they immediately started separating the wheat from the chaff, the strong from the weak, the fast from the slow. Anyone who fell behind the instructors at the back of the formation was immediately relieved of their class position and sent to another unit.

Once we arrived at the Black Top, an infamous location on the Ranger Compound where millions of push-ups have been done and even more "Fuck You"s have quietly been uttered, a pep talk worthy of a Bobby Knight halftime speech commenced.

"Forty percent of Rangers get wounded, fifteen percent get killed," the instructor said. "Y'all still want to be here? Great. If not, go the fuck home."

Standing out there in the shit Georgia weather with all the other newbies, these first words out of the instructor's mouth rang through the humid air like a gunshot. He wasn't trying to scare us, exactly; it was more about setting the tone. The next few weeks were going to be as hard and as shitty as any of us could imagine the vetting process would be for entry into a highly selective fighting force. Not just *anyone* gets to kill people and run into bullets, mmmkay? Instructors would be creating immense stress on a nearly constant basis to test our adaptability and leadership capabilities as we neared our breaking points. That's the real goal of RASP: to push you to the limit, to try to break you. To make you miserable every fucking second of the day so that you'll quit, because having someone in the Ranger Regiment who is susceptible to fear, physical exhaustion, or poor decision-making as a result of mental fatigue is like walking around with a land mine strapped to your ankle. There is no sense in sugarcoating it: Having some weak motherfucker in your unit will get you killed.

As the instructor kept talking, he added the next bit of stress, the next test for timidity and weakness. He made all of us hold our rucksacks above our heads. Even after our super shuttle to the Black Top, there were still too many students in the class. They needed to get rid of a bunch before they could start the course. So the first fifteen Airborne graduates to drop their rucks, well, they got a one-way ticket home.

I remember looking around and taking the measure of my classmates, studying their faces as the instructor's warnings resonated. Most of us had just gone through OSUT and Airborne together, so I figured everyone would be prepared for this last-man-standing test. I was wrong. Some guys were confused; others were plainly fearful. No matter how hard they tried, they couldn't hide it. As their arms shook under the weight of their rucks and their own estimations of themselves, you could see people calculating the odds in their head, questioning if they had what it took to keep going, to roll those dice, wondering if they should really be here. The number of guys who'd never even thought about quitting, let alone dying, between the time they enlisted and the time they got to RASP would blow your mind. It wasn't long before people started dropping their rucks, not because of physical fatigue but because of the reality check—I could *actually* die. Within thirty minutes, the instructors had their fifteen sacrificial lambs, and the rest—about forty to fifty of us—moved on.

The first week of RASP was less difficult than I expected, mostly because there wasn't much that was new. A lot of this initial week was just an extension of the previous twenty-week marathon suck-fest, except now the training was constant—twenty hours per day, every day. The real dick-twisting came during the second week when they sent us out to this awful, remote part of Columbus called Cole Range, which is a forest-lined swampland. If Columbus is the asshole of America, then Cole Range is those bloody little cuts at the top of the asshole that snag all the dingleberries when it gets hairy up there.

The real beauty and elegance of Cole Range isn't in the topography, it's in the timing. It doesn't signal the end of a training phase, like other brutal military rites of passage do. It's just there in the middle of everything to remind you that getting your dick kicked in the dirt for a week straight is probably going to be a regular part of your job—if you even make it, that is. The isolation, the constant companionship of only other dudes who are as miserable as you, that's just extra!

Most days at Cole Range, you're operating on two hours of sleep if you're lucky. Some days you march with eighty-pound rucks strapped to your back, not really sure where you're headed. Other days, the instructors capitalize on the exhaustion and constant chaos of training to throw all manner of ridiculous fuckery at you, just to see how you respond. It was at this point in my life that I learned to laugh at situations that were beyond fucked. I realized that there was no point in complaining about things that are outside of my control because no one would be listening, especially since I was the one who had volunteered for this shit in the first place.

In the middle of Cole Range, I would have killed for someone to bring clarity to my choices—*Why, Mat, did you agree to submerge yourself in gator-piss swamps at 4 A.M.?*—but instead, day after day, all I could do was laugh at everything and repeat to myself, "It's only a few more weeks." A few more weeks and I can finally sleep and be warm again. A few more weeks and I can eat a decent meal again. A few more weeks and maybe I can sweet-talk one of those Columbus Waffle House waitresses into a covered and smothered Best Hot Plate Special. (It's off the menu, available by request only.)

The worst part of the whole experience, at least for me, came on the very last night at Cole Range. It was early spring, and it had rained nearly every goddamn day. In Georgia, temperatures are still kind of cold this time of year. Every night we were out there, it felt like it dropped into the twenties. By sundown our uniforms would be soaked through with rain and sweat, only to freeze over like giant, stinking sweat-sicles by midnight if we didn't keep moving.

The good news, I guess, was that we rarely stopped moving. Every night, the instructors made you set up a patrol base in what was invariably the shittiest possible location to do so. It was a fun little exercise, like burpees on broken glass or listening to rich suburban college students from two-parent households talk about systemic poverty and social justice. On the last night, the instructors had us set up our patrol base in about a foot of standing water. I can still see the smiles on their faces as they looked at us, shivering and feeling like death.

"All right, Ranger Best, how about you sit the fuck down in it?" one of them said.

"Right here, Sergeant?" I asked, pointing down to the puddle of water.

"No, in your suite at the Doubletree. Yeah, right the fuck there! Is that a problem?"

"No, Sergeant, just *double*-checking." That joke, along with many, many others I told to cut the edge off the misery during the week, did not land well.

"The rest of you can join the comedian for open mic night. Everybody down in the fucking water," he said with the ease of a man versed in the subtle science of slow torture. "It's bath time!"

"All of us?" a guy in our class responded, almost pleading for any other kind of punishment. Come on, bro, you know the answer. We're Three Musketeer–ing this shit.

"Oh yeah, Sugar Bear. Snuggle up," the sergeant said.

At first, as we settled down in our waterbed, I was amazed that we might actually be able to steal a couple hours of shuteye. When you've been run this ragged, any time you're off your feet feels like an opportunity to sleep.

Then reality kicked in. Oh right, this stagnant-ass water is arctic cold.

It wasn't long before my entire class looked like a youth group at a Parkinson's convention. To a man, we were violently shaking. We had to do something or one of us was going to get hypothermia and fucking die in this Michael J. Foxhole. (N-n-n-nailed it.) The instructors were fully aware of that. They weren't just testing us to see if we could endure all this bullshit, they wanted to see if we could work together as a unit to unfuck ourselves.

That's when we decided to form a twenty-man cuddle buddy chain. Two guys would hold each other chest to chest, like mama and baby otters do, then we'd sit back to back with another pair of guys to limit the amount of surface area exposed to the air. I've never even hugged my own father with this much feeling, let alone someone I've known for less than a month, but I held on to the dude facing me like he was Hillary Clinton's emails—I was never letting go.

After a few minutes, the cuddle-buddy chain started working.

Then I had to piss. *Bad.* You forget about things like bodily func-
tions when you've been operating on adrenaline and no sleep for
multiple days in a row. It's only when you taste that first tiny mor-
sel of comfort and relaxation that the urge to empty out rushes to
the front of your mind. And when it comes, it comes with the fury
of a flash flood. When I started to disengage from my cuddle buddy,
a southern gentleman named Bishop, he grabbed ahold of my
shirt and pulled me back into him.

"Don't go," he said.

"I have to piss," I told him, trying to get him to unlatch.

"I don't fucking care," he said through shivering teeth, grabbing
on tighter.

"Dude."

"Just piss right here." The desperation in his eyes was palpable.
"Please, man, I need you."

"It's gonna get all over you."

"Good."

"What do you mean, 'good'?!"

"I want you to fucking piss on me." He nodded weakly, before
letting out one last breath that I could see dissipate into the Georgia night sky. "It'll be warm."

I looked into Bishop's eyes again. In that brief moment something
had changed in him. All the insecurity we try to hide when we're
young, all the macho posturing around sex and homosexuality and
masculinity, it was all melting away for Bishop right in front of me.
Any bit of shame or modesty or boundaries he had before this night,
that was all gone. And that was the whole point of the exercise. To
shed whatever bullshit defenses we had brought with us in order
to work together in the common defense and get the job done.

"Dude, that's kind of gay," I said. (Clearly, I still had some work
to do.)

"It's not gay if it's cold." Even through chattering teeth, Bishop
responded with such conviction that it sounded like he'd thought
about this for a while (and maybe even consulted with his pastor
just to be sure). The reality is, in the early stages of freezing your

balls off, the minutes pass like hours, and you have a lot of time to think. That gave Bishop more than enough time to rationalize the decision to turn himself into a human toilet.

"Do it right now, motherfucker. We need this for warmth."

The urgency in his voice was unnerving. I looked into his eyes one last time, probing for some kind of indication that maybe he was fucking around. Then I looked inside myself and realized what Bishop already knew. When you enlist in the United States Army, intent on joining one of the three battalions of the 75th Ranger Regiment, what you are really signing up for is a commitment to do whatever it takes, whenever and wherever it is asked of you. The men you will be fighting with are your brothers, and when they need you, you need to be there, no matter the cost, no matter the sacrifice. This guy might one day die in my arms, I realized. The least I could do was piss into his.

Against every instinct in my body, I accepted the situation for what it was and pissed on another man. This was no ordinary piss, either. This was like a Bruce Springsteen concert. It just kept going and going, and all I could do was sit there in awe, waiting and wondering, *Will this ever end?!?*

But I'll be goddamned if Bishop wasn't right. As I began to feel the trickle of regret fill my already-soaked camo bottoms, regret quickly turned into relief, in the form of 98.6-degree yellow liquid. This was the warmest either of us had been all week. If I had known earlier, I would have pissed myself every chance I had. I wouldn't even have bothered to pull my dick out of my pants all week, now that I think about it.

In the end, our cuddle chain never broke. We survived the rugged, fissured butthole that is Cole Range by clinging to each other like the dingleberries we were. No one could rip us apart; no one could wipe us out. We would be there, irritating the shit out of our instructors, the itch they couldn't scratch, all the way to RASP graduation two weeks later.

———

The most important moment of RASP, other than graduation, happens the day before, when you find out to which of the three battalions you've been assigned. Everyone had their personal preference for their own unique reasons, and with America engaged in a two-front war at the time, dudes were super anxious about where they were headed. Not surprisingly, a lot of guys wanted 2/75 once they heard that that battalion was next up in the deployment cycle.

Of course, the Army didn't even bother pretending to give a shit about anyone's preferences. All they did was split the whole graduating class into three sections, lined us up in formation, and randomly assigned each group to a battalion. My group got 3/75, right here in Columbus, the last pick on my list. *Well, fuck.* I tried to put my bad luck into context. Be happy that you passed, I told myself. You get to join one of the most prestigious units in the military, I reminded my deflated ego.

At this moment an instructor yelled out, "Best, you have orders to go to 2/75!"

Every man in the class turned toward me in confusion. No one else got *orders*, let alone orders to the place they actually wanted to go. *Who was this little cocky Private First Class named Best?* That was the question painted on everyone's faces, instructors included.

"Why the fuck do you have 2/75 orders?" a fellow graduate finally asked me, in total disbelief. What do you say to a stupid question like that? Something witty and insightful, obviously.

"I'm a Make-A-Wish kid. Ken Griffey Jr. must have been busy. This was my second choice," I said like a total dickhead.

"Fuck you, man."

"You won't get to, because I'll be deployed. Have fun trying not to get the Waffle House waitresses pregnant."

The next day, after graduation, I called my cousin.

"Hey man, I just wanted to thank you."

"For what?"

"For the orders to 2/75."

"No idea what you're talking about." Uh-huh.

"Okay," I said with a chuckle. "Sincerely, thanks, cuz."

"Good luck," he said as he hung up the phone. He was a man of few words, but for the few words he offered on that day back in Airborne School and whatever good words he used to get me assigned to 2nd Ranger Battalion, I was grateful. God knows that by getting those orders I pissed off more people that day than I pissed *on* the previous four weeks, and I was grateful to be on my way to Fort Lewis, and from there into combat in Iraq.

Chapter 5

A Soldier *Comes* Home

My first real break in the Army, on something called block leave, came after graduating from RASP and returning from my first combat deployment to Mosul.

Hey, Mat, wait, WTF? Did you just skip over your entire first tour of actual warfighting?

I did. I accomplished jack shit on that first deployment. The operational tempo of my unit was high, but as a cherry private I didn't get to do much of the cool stuff. On most missions, the more experienced guys kicked down the doors while I pulled security. I'd sit in the vehicle hearing flash bangs and gunfire, wishing I were a part of it. Then there were stretches of time where the closest I'd get to direct contact was when the Iraqis decided to lob mortars at our compound. Most landed short of the fence line, some sailed clear over us, but a couple landed on base. A few months earlier the enemy had mortared a mess tent on our compound during lunch, killing twenty-two and wounding sixty-six. They were clearly hoping that lightning might strike twice. The whole experience was frustrating, to be honest, because I had all this training and no chance to implement it fully. I felt like I was in the middle of a fight with both arms tied behind my back.

Anyway, block leave is basically an extended vacation that the military grants to an entire unit around the holidays and before and after deployments. It's their way of giving soldiers an opportunity to relieve some stress, reunite with family, and find new and unique ways to get in trouble without bringing the rest of their unit down with them.

I decided to spend my ten days of block leave back home on the beaches of Santa Barbara. I hadn't seen my family in forever, and for months on end I'd been living in a dirty, hellish, backward shithole—and then Iraq—which made me more anxious and grateful for the comforts of home than anything else I could do or anywhere else I could go.

The cliché about military homecomings is totally real, by the way. When I stepped off that plane, I did hug my parents a little tighter. There was lots of crying. I really was genuinely happy to be home with everyone. I felt like one of those suburban moms in Oprah's audience in that glorious, carefree period between getting a free new Toyota RAV4 and learning that I would have to pay $7,000 in taxes on it. Even more than spending time with my family, though, what I was most excited about was going out and seeing everyone from high school, because I had changed . . . *a lot*.

If you're anything like some of the people in my real life I've told about my high school botany and bass-playing experiences, I imagine it's hard to reconcile the rock-hard instrument of swift justice and All-American handsomeness you see before you today with the idea that I was once a complete fucking dork. But if you think *you're* having a hard time with it, just picture the reactions of the people I went to high school with when I walked into a house party that first night back home.

In my mind, I secretly hoped that the whole scene would play out like a Kid Rock video. Pot smoke surrounds me like it's coming out of a fog machine. I kick open the door to every room I enter. People's jaws hit the floor. Guys give me the *'sup, bro* head-nod, not as a form of acknowledgment but as a way of self-consciously making their chins look stronger and their necks look thicker— like mine had become. Girls' heads turn on a swivel. And all those "I don't have the time of day for you" girls from high school seem to have found an open slot for me in their Google calendars. Possibly one of them faints.

As cool as it would have been to the sensitive ego and wild fantasies of that insecure high school kid to have the party stop rotating on its axis the moment I arrived, the reality is that the world managed to keep turning while I was gone, and it would continue turning the same way when I was home. People were happy to see me, sure, but nobody lost their shit over me. Well, nobody except a good friend of mine named Ryan, who ended up bro-ing out a little too hard that first night.

He was that buddy you haven't seen in a long time who just keeps complimenting you like he's trying to hint at some kind of personal awakening that you missed while you were gone. It starts with the nod, then the full-body check-down, then the step-back and double-take. Our first conversation was so odd and surreal, all I remember clearly now is it feeling like one of those *Saturday Night Live* sketches where they take one joke and beat it into the ground for five minutes until not only is it not funny anymore but you question why you still watch that fucking show anyway.

"Holy shit, Mat, you're fucking ripped, dude," he said.

"Aww shit, thanks, man. Fucking military, right?"

"Yeah, man, definitely. Milk does a body good up in this motherfucker. You look *strong*, man."

"Thanks," I said, now feeling a tad uncomfortable.

"Hell, yeah! Like, really fucking strong, man. It's almost like you're a different person. You're like the Incredible Hulk now! I'm not even going to try and make you angry," Ryan shouted as he lifted his arms up above his face.

"Yeah, the military kind of molds you into great shape."

"No, I get it, be all you can be. I've seen the commercials, bro. It's just, damn, man, you look big. Like, *defined*, man." He reached in and started to squeeze my biceps. Not in a gay way. More in the Gold's Gym bro "your glutes look amazing" way.

Nope. I grabbed Ryan's hand and squeezed a pressure point. "We're all good on that," I said.

"Okay, man. Okay. Let go. I'm just playing an' shit." He laughed that kind of laugh where you're in legitimate pain, but you don't want to show the other person, because perversely, you still want them to like you.

In truth, the nature of Ryan's reaction wasn't all that unusual. I noticed it when my brothers came home from boot camp, too. It's a certain look you get from people—a mixture of admiration and apprehension. In one moment they're thinking, "Man, this guy has put in some work." In the next: "Man, I wouldn't fuck with this guy." Now it was happening to me, and it was weird, because when you're in the military, you don't really see your body changing that much. You're too busy being tired and getting yelled at to notice. And besides, every other dude looks like you, so nothing you see in the mirror seems all that impressive. It's not until you step away from it and you're back in civilian life that you have the opportunity to look around and notice, "Holy shit, I could probably kill everyone in this bar."

It's a nice feeling.

Where I really felt the change wasn't in my physique as much as in my attitude. That was my *real* problem in high school. I tried so hard to get laid when I wasn't flipping botany burgers or slapping bass that I acted like a total pussy around girls. My utter lack of self-confidence made me terrified of saying the wrong thing or doing anything that might overtly sabotage my chances. Little did I realize that all my worrying was the biggest cock-block of them all. No girl wants to fuck a guy who can't make a command decision. Now I didn't care one way or the other. I just wanted to have fun.

Two minutes into my conversation with my touchy-feely friend, one of the hottest girls from my graduating class, this smoke show named Anna, came up to say hello. I knew Anna enough to pick her out of a lineup, but back in the day our interactions never went much beyond a "hello" from me and a nice cold shoulder from her. It was time to repay the favor.

"Hey, didn't we go to high school together?" she asked.

"I don't know, maybe," I said as I turned back to Ryan.

"You're from here, right?"

"Yeah," I said, almost annoyed.

"Well, there's really only one high school in our town, so we had to have gone to high school together."

"Oh, cool. Then yeah, I guess we did. Small world or some shit." Sick burn. In my head, I was lecturing Anna like this was a public shaming on Twitter. Two hundred eighty characters of fuck you. How does it feel to have the shoe on the other foot for once, huh Anna? You're not in control of my happiness anymore. It was like an awkward class reunion, except I was third-grade Billy Madison after failing to spell *Rizzuto* in cursive: *I hate cursive and I hate all of you! I'm never coming back to school! Never!*

"Do you want to get out of here?" she asked, interrupting my train of thought.

Excuse me, what was that? Did this girl who iced me out all through high school just walk up to me out of nowhere and ask me to leave with her? But . . . why? The "cool guy" Mat Best façade dropped and the navel-gazer on the inside started to pick his head up. I almost didn't know what to do.

I took a sip of my beer and attempted to regain my composure.

"Where do you want to go?" Great question, Mat. Why don't you just ask her which hole the pee comes out of while you're at it?

"I literally could not give one single fuck," she said without missing a beat. "Wherever you're going, I'm going, so you get to decide."

Now that is patriotism.

The one thing Ranger Battalion drills into your head more than anything else is putting your thoughts and feelings aside in order to get the job done. This girl had just given me a mission. Screw tasks, conditions, and standards; I just needed to go hard on the "objective." It was time to execute. I chugged the rest of my beer, took her by the hand, and walked her right out of the party and into my car. No goodbyes, no fist bumps with old friends, there was no time for any of those pleasantries. There was only one objective now.

Within five minutes, we were driving down the PCH (Pacific Coast Highway) in the old family Buick in search of the perfect place to park and stare up at the moon and the stars over the vast Pacific Ocean. And to get naked. But first, that awkward stop at the gas station along the way to buy some condoms.

In the movies, this scene is always full of anxiety. The main character isn't sure which size or brand to get. He's worried that someone from his mother's church group might see him. Hopefully he has enough money. None of those were my issue. My problem was the stoner clerk behind the register.

"Fuck yeah, man. You getting some?" he said as I dropped the box of condoms on the counter. "I like it. Hey man, didn't we go to high school together?"

Fucking Santa Barbara. Everyone knows each other. The city is eighty square miles and has more than 80,000 residents, but late on a Saturday night when you're trying to get your fuck on, you'd think this place was Casterly Rock and I was Jaime Lannister.

"Cool, man, probably. Nice to see you. How much do I owe you?"

He peered out the window to get a look at Anna in the front seat of my car. "Oh shit! Are you fucking *her* tonight?"

"HOW MUCH ARE THE FUCKING CONDOMS?!"

I'd had enough of this shit. It was time to take control of the situation. I hastily opened my wallet, threw down a ten-dollar bill, and bolted out of there. Correct change was the least of my concerns at that point.

Along the PCH, there are a bunch of places to park by the beach, and at night they are virtually empty except for a stray camper or two that belong to surf bums and road-tripping retirees. I drove for a couple of miles until I found a spot that felt isolated enough and pulled in. I parked the car and fumbled with the radio. Anna grabbed my hand to stop me on the first station without static. It could have been Mexican *ranchera* music full of accordions and she would not have cared. This was the first moment I really paused to take a good look at Anna. She was still blond and five-foot-seven like I remembered, but she was also impressively fit and weirdly confident. There was no trace of the petty high school insecurities. She knew what she wanted.

She was not trying to get to know me or rekindle an old flame. She had been an ice princess toward me in high school. There was no flame to speak of. What she saw in me was not a future life partner but something much more elemental than that: She saw a fucking *man*.

That house party we'd just come from was full of boys. It wasn't their fault. They'd all graduated, most of them had stuck around Santa Barbara, some had maybe started college or were taking classes somewhere, others had bullshit jobs doing this or that, but none of them had actually *done* anything yet. I've gotten to know a bunch of beautiful women over the years that reminded me of Anna in various ways—I eventually married one—and the stories they all tell from this period in their lives are riddled with frustration from having to deal with idiot guys—with go-nowhere *boys*.

When Anna decided she wanted to hook up and she looked at me among all those other guys, what she saw was a dick dispenser attached to a returning war hero and a hardcore motherfucker in his prime. In reality, of course, nothing could have been further from the truth—I spent more of my first deployment cleaning shit out of toilets than I did pulling the trigger of my gun—but when the hottest girl you've laid eyes on in the last eighteen months is convinced you're Jason Bourne, you don't pretend to be Jason Alexander.

That night and into the early morning, we used every single condom in the box. Before I took her home, somewhere around 6 A.M., as the sun began to rise over the mountains behind us, I looked at this girl and thought about how different my life had become. The skinny emo geek everyone remembered from barely more than a year earlier was nowhere to be found. In his place sat a motivated, chisel-jawed Army Ranger with a boatload of confidence in his gut, an unfamiliar degree of comfort in his own skin, and twenty more pounds of muscle on his frame. Everything I could have ever envisioned about being in the military was coming true, and I still had nine more days of block leave to go through.

———

The next night, I went to another house party and hung out with the same group of friends, except for Anna, who wasn't there. The part of me that was starting to get used to this whole Captain America thing wanted to believe that she was at home, sitting on a bag of frozen peas, writing me love letters in her diary:

Dear Mat, I am so sorry for big-timing you back in "the high." Last night, while you were making love to all of my bathing suit parts, I finally felt what it's like to be a true American again. Like a real one, you know, like John Cena or Hank Williams Junior. I finally learned the error of my ways. You are a true hero. I would ask you to marry me like right now, except it would be selfish of me to rob the world of your touch. They say if you love something, set if free, and if it returns, then it's yours. I totally don't even care if you come back. You are like an eagle, like a wild stallion, like public restrooms in European cities. You need to be free. So go, Mat. Be free. Freedom your fucking face off! And fuck the freedom into anyone who stands in your way.

Girls talk like that, right?

I never got a chance to find out, because one of the cheerleaders from my class, a girl named Alexa, approached me early in the night and captured my attention. Side note: I'm still Facebook friends with her and she seems super happy with her husband now that the whole "Fuck my cheating husband" period has blown over.

Alexa never even knew I existed in high school, but on the heels of marathon animal sex the night before, my confidence meter had skyrocketed to a zillion, and none of those awkward social dynamics from the past meant a thing to me. Oh, to be young and dumb again.

"Hey, didn't we go to high school together?" she asked. Oh no, sister, you don't get to play coy with me. I turned to give her my full attention. I only had nine more days before I went back up to Fort Lewis. It was time to get down to business.

"Who gives a fuck about high school? You don't know me and I barely know you. Let's change all that tonight and try not to get pregnant. What do you say?" Pure romance.

"That's a little forward," she said through nervous laughter.

"Well, this truck ain't going *backward*. You down or what?"

Alexa was no idiot. You don't survive a vicious clique like a high school cheerleading team, having spent four years at the top of a human pyramid with everyone looking up your business, without knowing how to navigate the reputational threats that come from hooking up with random dudes. There was a process to this. There were expectations. She wasn't just going to lie down on the ground right there and pull her panties to the side. This wasn't *heaven*. This was a house party. Dignity was important.

"Let me say bye to my friends," she replied, glancing straight into my eyes for just a second. The fun, open, flirty look on her face from when she'd first walked up to me was gone. In its place was the certitude of a sexual Terminator. Through her fixed gaze, I could see that she'd done all the calculations. She'd assessed me, she'd assessed the environment, and she'd made her decision.

All my brain could muster was: *Oh, fuck, I can't believe that just worked.*

When she went over to say good night, I could see her recounting our conversation to all her gorgeous friends. They looked over at me and giggled. Some of their eyes grew wide in mock surprise. One of them smacked her on the ass as she walked back toward me, like a coach offering encouragement to her star running back as she headed back into the game on fourth and (a girthy eight) inches.

It was more than a little intimidating, because it was clear that this girl knew what she was doing (or was about to do), while I, without a ton of experience under my belt, had no idea—though I was learning fast. The only thing that came to mind was to make it a carbon copy of the night before. So I took her to the exact same beach lot and pulled into the exact same parking spot after going back to the exact same gas station for the exact same box of condoms.

The only thing missing was a case of Bounty paper towels, because this former cheerleader was a squirter, and by the time we were done there was a mess all over the backseat of the Buick, and, even worse, all our body heat and friction had baked it into the fabric. There was no way I could bring my parents' car home smelling like diluted girl pee. We're not Germans. I had to fix this.

At some point the sun started to rise over the mountains. That could mean only one thing: Home Depot was about to open. I dropped Alexa off back at the party house, where her car was parked, and then ran to the Depot to get some of that industrial-strength carpet cleaner they use at motel crime scenes. Right there in the parking lot, I got to scrubbing like Lady Macbeth.

I'm not complaining, I promise. I had no problem diving in and cleaning out that backseat. I was like a toddler who fingerpaints his bedroom walls with the poop from his dirty diaper and then stands back to admire it. Yeah, Mom, I did that. I made this mess. Or at least, I made her make this mess. I felt a tremendous sense of accomplishment.

A few nights later, as the parade of house parties marched on, I switched things up and left with a girl named Meg whom I barely remembered from high school. Meg was a year older than me. From a high school hierarchy perspective, there was nothing exceptional about her—she wasn't a Regina George type or a cheerleader or Megan-Fox-in-*Transformers* hot. Nothing that would have made her stick out in my memory. She was just a cool person who was fun to talk to that night and whom I knew about as well as anyone knows half the people they were friends with on MySpace. In essence, I liked her profile picture and wanted to slide into those PMs. Fortunately for me, her privates were not set to private, and by the end of the night she wanted to go back to her place so that I could put *My*Space into *Her*Space. I was excited, because I was getting kind of tired of fucking in my parents' car. There's only so much you can do in a sedan.

Spoiler Alert: Be careful what you wish for, boys and girls, because you just might get it.

There's something you need to understand about where I grew up: There are actually two Santa Barbaras. One is fabulously wealthy and posh, with huge homes, lush gardens, and amazing views. People like Oprah and Ellen DeGeneres and Tom Cruise have houses there. Sometimes people call it Montecito, other times they'll call it the American Riviera, and it's as beautiful as the pictures in the brochure. Then there is the Santa Barbara with houses that look like they washed ashore after an Indonesian tsunami fifty years ago and came to rest under some palm trees. That's the Santa Barbara I am from.

That's the Santa Barbara that Meg's house was in. If you even want to call it a house. It was so small that Meg and her family probably qualified as being homeless in the state of California. The whole thing couldn't have been more than 900 square feet.

When we got to the front door, she put her finger to her lips. "Keep it down when you walk inside, my parents are sleeping," she instructed me. Keep it down? I wasn't worried about waking them up with my voice, I was more concerned with stepping on them or hitting them with the door when we walked in.

"Okay, but won't they be able to hear us, you know, doing stuff?"

"No, we'll go out to the garage. My brother has it built up pretty cool. We'll be alone in there."

What is this place, the *Goonies* house? Is your brother Josh Brolin? Is he going to be in there fondling a chest expander and eye-fucking me? I had so many questions, but I put them all aside because Meg was going to let me trust-fall into her vagina, and insulting her home was a surefire way to fall on my face.

"All right," I said. "Lead the way."

We tiptoed through her dollhouse kitchen and she guided me into the garage, which she illuminated by pulling the string on a single forty-five-watt bulb suspended from an I-beam that held up the roof. I was right. It *did* look like the *Goonies* garage. There were posters of fast cars tacked to the exposed wall beams. There was even a shitty little weight bench with those old-school plastic plates that you have to fill with sand. Nothing about this room screamed "cool," even to a kid like me who had a résumé full of dork.

"How old is your brother, fourteen?"

"No, he's your age. He went to school with us," Meg said nonchalantly as she led me past the Fisher-Price weight bench.

"Oh, okay. So your parents just kept this sort of preserved for him?" I was trying to give him the benefit of the doubt.

"No, he still lives at home," she said. "He's staying at Steve's house tonight."

"Yeah, Steve. Cool," I said confidently. I don't know who Steve is and after the nickel tour I didn't really want to find out.

Apparently, knowing that Steve is a name that guys have was enough to put an end to the small talk. Meg quickly removes her top and leads me over to what appears to be a large pull-out futon bed with a huge comforter stretched over it. The comforter is tucked in around the sides on the concrete floor. No metal frame, no box spring, just floor. That's okay, though, I've slept on worse.

Meg sits downs gently and I hear a loud crunch. I take off my shirt and she extends her hand toward me.

"Just sit down carefully, okay?"

I have no idea what she is talking about, so I let her take the lead and guide me down on top of her, but when the weight of my body presses down, I feel a loud metal crunch, accompanied by the same noise she made when she sat down. She giggles like this shit is adorable. Like fucking inside a recycling bin is a turn-on.

"What is this thing? This doesn't feel like a futon."

"It's our old garage door," Meg says with a laugh. "My dad didn't really know how to dispose of it, so he's just kept it in here all these years. My brother uses it as a bed."

"Wait, you want to have sex on your brother's bed, which is actually your old garage door, that is *inside* your garage, which is covered by your current garage door?"

"Yeah. Why not?"

"You don't find that weird?"

"I've never really thought about it. We just have to be quiet—"

"—because we're having sex on top of an old metal door."

"Well, yeah," she says.

As I take off my jeans, I can hear and feel every single crunch from the garage door. Part of me is terrified that we'll wake up her parents; another part of me wants to yank back the comforter to get a look at this thing. Meg insists it's a garage door, but to me it sounds like a giant potato chip bag full of tetanus. When we finally get all of our clothes off and I put a condom on, it sounds like a tornado in a tin can. The metal garage door is being less forgiving of our movements than a tight satin dress in high definition. There is no hiding anything. At first I go slow, trying to muffle as much noise as I can, but instead of a tornado now there's this eerie creaking sound echoing through the room, like a crab boat trying to cut through the Bering Sea ice pack.

"You can go faster," she whispers in my ear. "My parents' room is on the other side of the house. They'll never be able to hear us."

"Are you sure?" I ask. I'm not buying it. Jiminy Cricket slept in a matchbox that was bigger than this fucking house.

"Oh, totally," she says, as if she's gone the distance on top of this garage door plenty of times. The idea that her sexual sample size is statistically significant enough to make a confident claim like this is a little unnerving, I'm not going to lie. Not because it makes me think less of her. To the contrary, it makes me think less of myself. I don't have the bedroom reps that she has (though technically neither does she if she spent all of high school hooking up on top of a door). If I don't find my groove on this thing, I'm going to blow it and be totally disappointing. This is not how I want to end block leave.

Goddammit, Mumblecore Mat, get both your heads in the game!

I start to pick up the pace. Eventually, my body adjusts to the grooves of the metal door, and not only am I able to get good leverage, but I find a really good rhythm and we all start to feel like we're moving as one—me, Meg, and the door. It's virtually symphonic. Then, just as I'm about to orgasm, I hear a loud noise, followed immediately by a bright light. The actual garage door is going up on us.

"Oh shit!" Meg says, panicked. "I think my brother is home!"

"What do you mean *home*? It's a garage."

Now she looks at me like *I'm* the crazy one. That's when it dawns on me: *He really does live in this fucking garage.* For a total shitbox of a house, the garage door goes up surprisingly fast. The way the makeshift bed is positioned, we're the first thing her brother is going to see. The glare of his car's headlights hit us right in the face. We try to grab for our clothes, but to no avail.

"Meg?"

"John, I can explain," she says as she awkwardly pulls the comforter over her chest. As the garage door comes to a rest and the headlights finally turn off, I see two pairs of men's legs.

"What the fuck are you doing in my room?" he asks angrily.

"To be fair, it is the *garage*," I interject.

"Wait, weren't you in that emo band?" his friend asks.

"Ha, I was."

"Shut the fuck up, man," John says. "Meg, get out of my fucking room."

"Fine. Could you at least close the garage door and give us a second? God!" Meg says as she fumbles around for her clothes.

John hits the garage door remote and, as it slowly closes, I can hear his friend. "Hey, man, their band was actually pretty good," he says, cracking himself up.

If I hadn't already been red-faced from fucking, I would have totally blushed as we got dressed. I couldn't *believe* he recognized me from my Blind Story days. I had no idea that someone might remember us. I was genuinely touched by that—even if they did ruin our episode of *Casting Garage*.

Believe it or not, this was the perfect way to end a week and a half of blissful, rugged sex. Getting on the plane to Tacoma, Washington, back to my unit to prepare for our next deployment, I was filled with even more purpose than I had had before the first one.

I was feeling a new sense of confidence, and I was ready to get back overseas and finally get into the *real* combat I had been dreaming about for the last two years.

That's the funny thing about dreams, though. The fun is in the chasing. Once you achieve them, they usually don't give you the sense of satisfaction or gratification that you had thought they would. Sometimes you realize you were really chasing something else all along. And then other times, like I was about to find out, they have a fucked-up way of bringing you back down to reality.

Chapter 6

Brehm and Barraza

A mere twelve months after joining the Army, I was back in Iraq for the second time with the 2nd Ranger Battalion. My hope for my second deployment was to finally apply all my war-fighting skills and see real war firsthand. I thought there was a good chance this might happen because my unit got surged forward ahead of standard rotation and was told that we'd be hitting the ground running. That doesn't happen unless things are really starting to get chippy, right?

I'll never know for sure, but I think my team leader, Sergeant Dale Brehm, felt the same way and understood how different this deployment might be for me. As we prepared to deploy, he pulled me aside one day and gave me a big piece of news: When we rotated home at the end of this six-month deployment, it would be my turn to go to Ranger School—I had made the cut to attend the combat leadership course and to keep progressing within the unit.

Brehm also gave me his Ranger tab and Ranger scroll. In Ranger tradition, you sew your team leader's tab and scroll into the inside of your PC (patrol cap), and whenever shit gets really hard, whenever you have doubts or feel like you're hitting a wall during the training, you can take off your PC and look at those patches as a reminder that you have what it takes to make it to the end of the suck, and that the guy who gave you those patches thinks so too. Someone had done that for Sgt. Brehm before he went through Ranger School, and now he was paying it forward to me.

His gesture and the confidence that he showed in me really buoyed me as we arrived in late October 2005 and headed toward a border region called Anbar Province, renowned as a major artery for the inflow of foreign fighters from Syria. Our area of operation had just seen a major American offensive clear through it. We were tasked to find the remaining fighters and kill or capture them, which wound up being easier than I had anticipated.

Once we got situated and fully operational, we conducted raids every night for weeks on end without finding ourselves in any kind of major engagement. Partly that was because the offensive that preceded us had done a pretty good job. But I suspected that the primary reason we were coming up empty-handed was because it was getting into winter and the fighting season over there is during the warmer months. You don't go to Aspen in July looking to ski, right? Well, you don't come to Iraq in December looking to fight.

As the deployment dragged on, we'd go out on an operation, get on target, and any bad guys who were still there would surrender immediately. (I called them cold-weather quitters.) The cadence of it all during this period of the fighting in Iraq became so reliable that, even if we were in a particularly concentrated area, we could blitz through multiple targets in a night—sometimes up to a dozen. It was like old-fashioned blitzkrieg, but with smaller units and bigger beards. My platoon was not unique in this regard—it was happening to special operations units all over the country— it just pissed me off maybe more than the others because I wanted to get in gunfights, not earn a merit badge in zip-tie knots.

Even though coalition forces were bagging some big players in the Global War on Terror at the same time, that offered me no solace, because my interests were not geopolitical. They were visceral. I wasn't obsessed with winning; I was obsessed with the act of *war*. That's what I was there for, and that's what I wanted to be good at.

This wasn't some kind of fucked-up bloodlust, but it was very primal. At its most basic, war is a *mano a mano* fight to the death in service of something much bigger than yourself. General Douglas MacArthur called it "Duty, God, Country" in a speech to cadets at West Point near the start of the Vietnam War. Shakespeare called it a "band of brothers." Whatever you want to call it, to fight in its defense is the ultimate test—a test I was desperate for the opportunity to face and anxious to pass. As a nineteen-year-old kid, I wasn't smart enough to understand why this drove me so hard, and to a degree I still don't fully get it, but what I do know is that I was not alone. Humans and other mammals have engaged in some version of battle in defense of territory, family, the pack or the tribe, for hundreds of thousands if not millions of years. Today, "educated people" like to think we've evolved beyond this fundamental instinct, and they look down their noses at warfighters as primitive or regressive (whatever the fuck that means), but all you need to do is spend two minutes on Twitter to realize that this ancient animal impulse is alive and well.

Still, there is a danger in giving yourself over too completely to the thrill of war, and I was coming very close to crossing that line before I'd even fired a fatal shot. The danger is not that you will lose yourself, though that is always possible, but that you will lose sight of the greater purpose of each mission. On this second trip there were times when I didn't fully appreciate the danger of some of the situations that we were inserting ourselves into night after night, what with our crazy high operational tempo. I was never reckless, but there were times when I wasn't necessarily seeing the full field, and when that happens, bad things can follow.

Those first few months, we were blowing down doors and dodging bullets nearly every night, but it never really felt like we were being tested too badly—at least not beyond what our training had prepared us for—so it never felt like I'd been able to take my training wheels off to see what I was really made of.

Then, with two months left on the six-month trip, things started to change. We were re-deployed 250 kilometers to the southeast, to a city called Ramadi.

At this stage of the war, the vibe in Ramadi was totally different.

In recent weeks the insurgency had been getting pretty nasty in that area and the place had turned into a fucking tinderbox, one that would explode a couple months later as the Second Battle of Ramadi—a six-month pitched battle that involved the famous Task Unit Bruiser led by Jocko Willink of SEAL Team Three. It's also where Chris Kyle got his nickname "The Devil of Ramadi." Ramadi produced dozens of American casualties, a Medal of Honor recipient, and God knows how many bronze and silver stars. Many brave Americans sacrificed a lot on those streets. And unlike the insurgents my unit encountered in and around Anbar, the fighters infesting the streets of Ramadi were willing to stand their ground and fight to the death.

I learned that fact firsthand during one of the first raids we conducted in our new AO (area of operation). The Stryker (an eight-wheeled armored fighting vehicle) my squad was riding in was repositioning to track down some enemy combatants that had just run from a target building. As we sped down an alleyway, one of them cooked off a command-detonated IED. *Well, this is new*. The explosion blew off two of our vehicle's front tires and stopped us in our tracks. Thankfully, no one was severely injured. We all kind of looked around, made sure our dicks were still intact, and gave a "Roger Up." Good to go.

Much of the next few weeks were just like that: testy, dynamic engagements, random gunfire from afar, IEDs here and there. Then, the week before we were set to leave and rotate back to the United States, we got a TST (time-sensitive target) out in some farmland west of the city. Initially, I didn't think much of it, but when we learned that the target was a transient house for foreign fighters making their way into Ramadi, my spidey sense started to tingle. This wasn't going to be a normal mission—I could feel it. Not that you can ever really put your finger on "normal" in the middle of a war, but something about this objective felt unsettled.

When we finally got spun up, I found myself in the middle of the helicopter between Sgt. Brehm and my squad leader, Sgt. Ricardo Barraza. These guys were two of the most legitimate badasses in the battalion. Within the tight-knit Ranger community, they were legends. But more personally, they had basically raised me since my first deployment, and I considered them family. When I showed up to the battalion with training but no combat experience, they strived to teach me what it truly means to be a Ranger: how to think, how to fight, how to carry yourself. And if the reactions of my friends to how much I'd changed when I returned home on block leave after that first stint in Mosul were any indication, Brehm and Barraza had been great mentors.

On this mission, we had good, timely intelligence that our target was holed up somewhere inside one of four buildings that were a solid six-kilometer infil from the HLZ (helicopter landing zone). We were in full kit, which meant we were each rolling up with eighty to a hundred pounds' worth of gear on us. I still remember that ruck so vividly. We were headed to what turned out to be a big farm in this quaint little village that is probably as close as Iraq will ever get to *Little House on the Prairie.* Almost immediately, we found ourselves amidst the worst possible terrain for fighting and stealth movement—a poorly maintained patchwork of plots segmented by these weird crumbling plow rows that prevented us from going straight toward the target for any meaningful distance before having to weave around one thing or climb over something else. In a few spots, we had to place ladders over open trenches just to get to walkable ground. By the time we reached the outskirts of the village and set up our ORP (operational reference point), nearly every member of the team had eaten shit at least once on the uneven ground.

With four buildings to hit, the ground force commander quickly delegated which target buildings were first and which squad would be assaulting each. The intelligence that we had indicated that the bad guys, if they were still there, were most likely to be in one or two of the four structures, so we broke up the unit into two assault squads and two support squads and decided to hit the buildings simultaneously. When everyone was clear on the plan, my squad began maneuvering toward the first building. I was uncomfortable from the moment we entered the village. The walls were low-cut and close together, with very little space between buildings. We had to walk in single file, making it tactically challenging to maneuver. We immediately found ourselves in a compromised position, and that is no way to start your approach.

Our target was a rudimentary Iraqi village house. It was 1,200 to 1,400 square feet at most, the walls were made of mud-based concrete, and the floors inside were almost certainly going to be filthy, hard-packed mud as well. We decided to set an ECT (explosive cutting charge) and go in loud while 2nd Squad took down the other building. As far as we knew, no one had any idea we were there.

As we entered the first room of the house, an enemy combatant bolted toward a bookshelf in the corner. I cut an angle on the room to clear my barrel from Sgt. Brehm and moved to squeeze the trigger to engage. Then, in what felt like milliseconds before I let the first round go, he suddenly stopped, put up his hands, and kneeled on the floor.

For some reason I couldn't explain, I didn't fire immediately. I felt like I still needed to give these people the benefit of the doubt, no matter who they were. This guy was giving up, so I had to let him give up. Saying those words again to myself more than a decade later, they sound so foreign. Twenty-two-year-old Mat would have blown this fucking guy's head off. But for nineteen-year-old Mat, even for all of his obsession with war and with killing bad guys, it wasn't so black-and-white. Plus, when you're confronted with this crazy situation for the first time, it's completely unnerving. You aren't thinking about the lights going out on the enemy or how you are going to tell this story in a book someday. All you're really trying to do is to see the full picture and make the correct decisions so that you and your brothers can get back home safe.

When I got up closer, that's when I saw the AK-47 on the shelf, well within arm's reach. Fortunately, Brehm saw it first and tackled the guy, then beat the shit out of him until I grabbed the weapon, locked and cleared it, and had a teammate zip-tie him so we could continue moving through the rest of the building.

The main guy we were looking for was not in this first building. We quickly moved outside and cordoned off one of the other buildings where we thought he was most likely to be. With the exterior secured, we began conducting a callout. A callout, in the most basic form, is when you have your interpreter yell out to anybody who might be in the building that shit is about to go down and they have two choices: Give up or die.

"Come out of the house!" the interpreter shouted. "The soldiers will kill you if you don't. Come out of the house or you will die!" He repeated himself four or five times for good measure. "This is your last chance before we begin firing!"

Those were the magic words. In a matter of seconds, it was like Ali Baba and all forty of his thieves came filing out of that house. It was the most bizarre thing I'd ever seen. Usually you see four, *maybe* five people—the normal size of an Iraqi family—come out of a structure this size. In this instance it was an Iraqi clown car. I counted sixteen of them before I lost track.

"Is there like eight bunk beds in each room," I asked one of the older men, through our interpreter, as he filed past me, "or are you guys just physically sleeping on top of each other?"

He just looked at me. No response. Typical.

"Is there anyone else inside this house?" my platoon sergeant asked a girl he had pulled aside.

"No," she responded via the interpreter.

"If there's someone in there, we're going to fucking kill them. Do you understand? You have to tell me if there's anyone else left inside."

"No, there's no one else inside. I promise." She was emphatic.

My platoon sergeant wasn't satisfied. He pulled a male in his twenties out of line and off to the side. "Is there anybody else in this building, because if there is we're going to blow up the whole fucking house. You got it?"

"No, no. I swear by Allah, there's no one else in this house," he answered.

Today, there is a way to find out for sure if they are telling the truth: You send in one of the working dogs. Run a fully trained, battle-hardened Belgian Malinois through that house and you'll find out real quick just how empty it is. Back then, however, canines and side plates and other protective measures were not a regular part of the SOPs (standard operating procedures) for missions like this, so you had to gather information on the fly and then go with your gut.

After everyone swore up and down that there was no one left in the building, we decided to do the charitable thing and return the line of bullshit they were feeding us. We split my assault squad into two teams. Bravo Team went to the black side of the building (the back side), while Alpha Team—which I was in—went to the white side (the front entrance). We decided to offset our breach so Alpha Team could go in slightly ahead of Bravo Team on the black side.

Boom. In.

As the dust settled from the door breach, we threw in a flash bang to disorient whoever might be waiting for us and entered into what appeared to be a tiny vestibule separating the front door from a reasonably large living room. On the other side of the room, across from the front door, we could see a staircase that led directly up to the second floor. We could also see a boatload of bad feng shui. To the left and right were parallel sets of closed doors that led to adjoining rooms. We had to clear those before moving upstairs.

Brehm and Barraza took the door on the left. Peters, another member of my team, locked down the staircase, which appeared to be barricaded at the top. My teammate Hansen and I took the door on the right. We breached our doors simultaneously. Very quickly my white light intersected with Hansen's and we called the room clear. As soon as those words left our mouths, the distinct and deafening sound of fully automatic fire rang out behind us. As Hansen and I tried to figure out where the sound was coming from, the chaos of nonstop gunfire in those few seconds scrambled our senses. It felt like being in a hall of mirrors made out of noise. A moment later, we realized that the gunfight had erupted inside the room that Brehm and Barraza had just entered.

Then we heard a faint voice.

"I'm hit. I can't move." It was Brehm.

Immediately, Hansen and I pushed through the living room, following Brehm's voice. We found him lying two or three feet inside the doorway of the adjacent room. He wasn't moving. As we tried to pie the room to gain better visibility, that's when we saw Barraza on the far side of the room. He wasn't moving either.

The speed at which all of this had taken place left Hansen and me momentarily disoriented and unsure of the proper course of action. We weren't even clear on what exactly had happened.

"I'll pull security, do you think you can grab Brehm?" Hansen said.

"Roger," I responded.

I jumped into the room, completely exposing my body. Hansen was pulling security, but with no line of sight into the room, I was sure a stream of bullets was going to rip through the side of my body. *But I'd rather die than not give aid to my teammate.* I grabbed a firm hold of Brehm's shoulder strap and the pull strap on the back of his kit and yanked him out of the room as hard as I could.

Somehow I exited the room unharmed and was able to pull Brehm back with me into the living room. I looked down at him and began an initial scan of his body for any obvious damage, but I couldn't find any. At this point, Brehm was nonresponsive, so I started to run scenarios through my head.

He probably just took a shot to the helmet. Or maybe the chest plate. It knocked him unconscious. Okay, that makes sense. He's good.

Next I started to undo Brehm's plate carriers to do a full medical sweep and search more thoroughly for any wounds. That's when he exhaled a mouthful of blood.

Goddammit. Goddammit. Goddammit.

At twenty-three years old, five-foot-nine, and maybe 185 pounds, Sergeant Dale Brehm was a fireplug and the consummate team leader. He always had us prepared for any situation. And he'd told us many times that if he was ever wounded, we should key his mic to call in help. So that's what I did.

"Medic, we need a medic in building 10!" I shouted through his push-to-talk.

Before I could release the button on Brehm's radio, automatic fire opened up on the opposite side of the building. Bravo Team had just made entry from the black side and engaged an enemy combatant, killing him as they cleared their way to us. When they finally entered the living room, Peters had joined Hansen pulling security as I attempted to administer first aid to Brehm. Our platoon medic, who followed Bravo Team in, immediately dropped to his knees next to me.

"Where is he hit?" the medic shouted.

"I'm not sure, he has no exposed wounds, but he's exhaling blood," I replied, as the medic began to work.

I jumped to my feet, realizing that we still had no understanding of what or where the threat was. At that point, another squad from our platoon arrived and we began preparing to stage on the room where Barraza's body was still lying motionless. The only portion of the room we couldn't see was the far back left quadrant, so the front member of our team tossed his flash bang in that direction. *Boom.* I followed him and another team member in. As the white lights of our weapons intersected, we saw a man lying underneath prayer mats, trying to hide, holding an AK-47 in his hand.

We all engaged with a flurry of gunfire, killing him immediately, although he may have already been mortally wounded.

With the immediate threat neutralized, we turned back to our wounded. We had two Rangers down. Two of our leaders. Two guys who gave everything they had to every mission and would give their lives to protect every man in their command. We needed to get them on a medevac as soon as possible. As this reality began to sink in, I let my emotions get the best of me.

"You motherfucker!" I yelled as I began to pummel the dead body of the insurgent with my fists. "You fucking piece of shit!"

I was wearing my carbon fiber gloves, and they began fracturing every part of the dead combatant's face. I could feel his orbital bones caving back into the soft tissue of his head. It was a feeling unlike any I had felt, before or since.

"Best, that's fucking enough, let's go," a squad member yelled at me.

I wish I could sit here and tell you, all these years later, that I should have been able to keep it together in that moment, that I should have understood that my desire to kill these dickheads was reciprocated by their desire to kill me, and that this was just the nature of war. But you know what? Fuck that. If I could travel back in time, I would change the course of that night just to make him feel every punch while he was still alive.

As my platoon began to regroup, we prepped Brehm and Barraza for the medevac. The Black Hawks were ten minutes out. We needed to pre-stage the casualties and get them to an open field about three hundred meters away that we'd designated as the HLZ. One team loaded Brehm on a stretcher and began moving him. Barraza wasn't so simple.

Twenty-four-year-old Staff Sergeant Ricardo Barraza was six-foot-two, 220 pounds, and a PT (physical training) stud of the highest order. Whatever the Spanish for "brick shithouse" is, he was that. Several weeks earlier, our base had held a giant flag football tournament. Our Ranger platoon fielded two twelve-man teams, one of which was led by Barraza. The rest of the teams in the tournament came from the *four companies'* worth of Marines, about six hundred men total, stationed there along with us. Barraza was not going to let a bunch of Marine infantrymen outperform Rangers. In his mind, it wasn't even an option. So he did what he always did: He went balls-out and won the whole fucking thing. He was an animal. He played with his team until 3 P.M. or so, then got some rest, got some chow, and was ready to go out on a mission by 10 that same night.

Now that unstoppable, immovable force of a man was lying at our feet. Like Brehm, he was unconscious and nonresponsive. It took a group of us to hoist him off the deck and get him onto a stretcher. As we began to make our way outside to the HLZ, I bumped into my best friend in the unit, Trey Bullock.

"I thought you were fucking dead, dude," he said gravely.

"Naw, man, it's Brehm and Barraza. They got hit, but we're going to get them out of here."

"You guys need extra security?" Trey said as he positioned his SAW (squad automatic weapon) toward the HLZ.

"We could use it, brother."

Trey tapped my helmet as if to say, "Good, because you're not going alone." Just ten minutes earlier, amidst the chaos of a close quarters gun battle, I struggled to understand what was happening, but now, in the swirl of a different kind of uncertainty, it was clear as day what I was in the middle of: true brotherhood. Live or die, now and forever.

With Trey at my side, we made it out to the HLZ just as the Black Hawks were landing. The dust off the rotor wash kicked dirt all over us, so we shielded Barraza with our bodies to protect him from the debris. As the wheels touched down, we sprinted to load him up, positioning him in the cabin of the helo with the help of the flight crew. Our medic relayed the medical information to the flight medic, and as soon as the helo landed it was wheels up and headed back to the FOB (forward operating base). An uncomfortable sense of relief set in as Brehm and Barraza disappeared into the night and Trey and I started running back to help clear and button this thing up so we could *all* get the fuck out of there.

That's when we heard a large explosion rip through the second target building, obliterating our brief sense of relief. We sprinted back and made it to the entrance in under a minute, though it felt like forever. When we pushed open the front door, we found members of our platoon laid out and bloody on the floor of the same living room I'd pulled Brehm from about fifteen minutes earlier. This fucking room was really starting to piss me off.

Here's what had happened. As our teams prepped and moved Brehm and Barraza to the HLZ, other teams were performing secondary clears, a process by which you move through a building room by room, checking any and all hiding spots for people, weapons caches, rigged explosives, you name it. Hidden inside an armoire in the room where Brehm and Barraza had been shot, my platoon sergeant ███████████████████████████████

███████████████████████████ discovered a boy who looked about fourteen years old. They demanded that he put his hands up, reluctant to engage the unarmed boy. Seconds later, the boy detonated a suicide vest. All five team members in the room at the time—three Rangers, the ███████████, and a Navy SEAL EOD (explosive ordnance disposal) tech—were wounded as the suicide vest packed with ball bearings exploded through them. Barely forty minutes into our time on target, 20 percent of our platoon had been wounded, some of them badly. We desperately needed to exfil off this patch of blood-stained dirt. But first we had to get these newly wounded brothers medevac'd.

As we gathered medical supplies to triage the wounded as best we could, we assessed the severity of their injuries. Two were only moderately wounded, including my platoon sergeant, who had taken shrapnel to the face and arms. While ugly, most of the lacerations were superficial, so he didn't miss a beat maintaining command and control of the platoon. Immediately he called in another medevac for the three others in the room who were more severely hurt. That's when we realized that we didn't have enough stretchers to get them off target and out to the HLZ.

The ground force commander instructed the incoming helos to adjust: They were to hover above the target building and drop off more stretchers before making their way to the HLZ to pick up the wounded. It wasn't long before the sound of a CH-47 Chinook helicopter churned through the air. I sprang up the stairs to the rooftop of the building and joined an element already pulling security as the massive, hulking twin-rotor bird hovered ten feet off the deck. The crew chief signaled a thumbs-up and dropped two stretchers onto the rooftop.

As we loaded the three most severely injured onto the stretchers, I spotted Hansen sitting against a wall. He had ball bearings in his leg and a completely shattered foot. Of my four-man Alpha team, I was now the only non-casualty. It was pure luck, though at the time it felt more like a curse.

Hansen watched as his more seriously wounded teammates were lifted and stretchered to the HLZ. "Of course, I'm going to have to walk my ass out of here, aren't I?" he said. It wasn't a question. He stood up on his good leg and hobbled toward the HLZ, in true Ranger fashion.

After hauling our Navy SEAL EOD counterpart to the HLZ (he had also taken multiple ball bearings throughout his body and suffered a significant fracture of his arm), I was finally able to link back up with my platoon and exfil. As I sat crammed in between my teammates and some enemy combatants we had taken off target, a mix of emotions rushed through my head: hate, vengeance, and strongest of all, disbelief. I was in the same position where I'd sat on the helo ride into the target earlier that night. From nearly this exact vantage point only a few hours before, I'd watched Barraza, with night vision goggles lighting up his eyes, stare out over the moonlit Iraqi terrain. I didn't know what he'd been thinking about, but I knew it was good and it was just, because I *knew* Ricardo Barraza. Now, as I blinked to clear the blood-sweat out of my eyes, in that brief flash, I could see that moment all over again. It was a moment that was gone as soon as it happened, but it was one that seared itself into my consciousness, a memory that would never fade.

We returned to base just after 6 A.M., later than usual, and were immediately debriefed. That was when we learned, officially, that Sergeant Dale Brehm, twenty-three, and Staff Sergeant Ricardo Barraza, twenty-four, had been killed in action, doing what they loved for something they believed in, something greater than themselves. Duty, God, Country. Their band of brothers.

They died honorably, but their deaths were no less tragic to the people who loved them. Dale, who got his Ranger tab on September 10, 2001, would have had his twenty-fourth birthday coming three days later. Ricky was going to get married just weeks after we got back. Both men, who had grown up less than three hours away from each other in the Central Valley in California and joined the Army out of high school like the rest of us, were on their *sixth* tours.

About a week later, I was stateside to bury one of my mentors and my friends. As the honor guard carried Dale Brehm across the rolling grounds of Arlington Cemetery to his final resting place beneath a temporary white cross driven into the earth, I made certain to remember the things about him and Ricky that I admired most. I wanted to fuse these things into my character and make sure their legacies lived on in my heart and in my actions. I recommitted myself on a daily basis to my family, the way Dale had when he gave all his focus to his wife when they were together. I resolved to become a better warrior and an even better man, following Barraza's fearless example in the face of adversity.

Dale Brehm and Ricardo Barraza went down fighting that March night, each one, in his own way, saving my life. Their sacrifice will forever be my motivation to live. But more immediately, it would be my inspiration to double-time it down to Ranger School only a few short days later and work to become the kind of leader they showed me it was possible to be. Godspeed, brothers.

Chapter 7

Tab on the Shoulder,
Tats on the Sleeve

Ranger School is a two-month combat leadership proving ground open to all branches of the military, but the 75th Ranger Regiment is the only unit that requires all of its officers and non-commissioned officers to attend the course. It is broken into three phases—Darby, Mountain, and Florida—starting back in the butt-hole of America and dripping down into its taint by the time it's all said and done.

Darby, which takes place in a remote corner of Fort Benning in Columbus, is often called the "crawl" phase of Ranger School, because you have to crawl before you can walk. In other words, instructors basically become the worst parents ever and treat you like you're the baby who should have been a blowjob but who has ruined all of their life plans instead—and now they're going to make you pay for it. They don't let you sleep, they shove you to the ground all day long, and they scream at you with colorful words like "cocksucker" and "titty boy." It's like a depressing episode of *COPS* except you also get to learn the fundamentals of squad-level mission planning, which are the basic building blocks of Ranger leadership. If you can't lock in this stuff, then you weren't meant to lead men—or at least not yet—and you had a quick trip home ahead of you.

I would be lying if I said I wasn't nervous going into Ranger School, having come straight from Arlington Cemetery and Ramadi before that. Under normal circumstances, Rangers deploy once after RASP on a kind of probationary status to determine if they have what it takes, then go straight to Ranger School to get the tab and become a full member of the Battalion. But because 2/75 got surged forward before I could go, I ended up deploying twice as a probationary private before my chance to attend Ranger School came up. You'd think going in with all that experience would be an advantage—and to an extent I'm sure it was. It certainly kept my mind busy and focused on my goals, partly as a way to avoid getting caught up in my grief over losing Brehm and Barraza. But the benefit of going in six months earlier, after just one deployment, young and cherry, is that you still have the bliss of ignorance. You don't truly understand, in a visceral way, the real-world implications of what you're being taught. It's not all fun and games, obviously, but it's also not exactly life and death. After two deployments, which taught me the cold realities of war, I fully appreciated the stakes associated with mission planning. I knew what happened when shit went sideways, and I did not want to be the kind of soldier who might fuck that up.

More than anything, I did not want to disappoint Sgt. Brehm, wherever he may be. He knew I'd make it home, he knew I'd make it to Ranger School, and he knew I'd make it through. It was his job to know that, both as a Ranger team leader and as a leader of men. There was only one thing that Dale didn't anticipate on my behalf: flesh-eating bacteria.

Listen, I could go into the many challenges that Ranger School presents, or you could Amazon the other eighty "how to be a Ranger" books that probably exist. This isn't a fucking self-help book, okay? And this isn't a chapter about the rigors of training. It's about how impressive it is that the only infection I got came not from the multitude of sex acts I've committed but from Ranger School itself.

In Florida Phase, which is the real fun one, you conduct small water operations, small craft movements, and platoon-sized operations, all in an awful Florida swamp on Eglin Air Force Base, situated strategically along the picturesque Redneck Riviera. Those last three weeks of Ranger School are where you learn just how much you want that Ranger tab on your left shoulder, because that entire stretch stinks like a bag of smashed assholes that has been left to rot in a Wal-Mart parking lot in the middle of July—which is exactly when I was there.

Every day you're wading chest-deep into a scum-infested river, over and over again, using what the Army calls, in a hilarious bit of sadistic understatement, "expedient stream crossing techniques." I can tell you from firsthand experience, what we crossed every day *was not a goddamn stream.* A stream is something you and your girlfriend hop over to reach a meadow for a breezy little weekend picnic. In the rushing nightmare the Army had constructed for our navigating pleasure, you were lucky to keep your boots attached to your feet, because each step across the "stream" sucked them a little bit deeper into the swampy mud bottom. The true bliss of all of this training was knowing that *I would never be in a fucking swamp in Iraq.* (Great foresight, Army, getting rid of Desert Phase, BTW.)

Once you're across and back on land, the instructors can finally get back to smoking you like a fat nug of sticky kind bud: fast, hot, and straight to the bottom of the bowl. They don't care that you are wearing the least comfortable clothing known to man. *Oh, it's constantly wet and sticking to your body? It's covered in algae and alligator shit? That's great, why don't you go back across that stream with your full ruck on and tell someone who gives a fuck?* They try to make every single waking second of Florida Phase uncomfortable for you. When they know they're succeeding, there is a lot of laughter to be had at your expense. Meanwhile, as they laugh, your exhausted, delirious, sun-stroked brain starts to concoct all the different ways you might be able to kill these sonsabitches in their sleep. If you could have stepped inside my head in those moments, you could have *Minority Report*-ed me right to a maximum-security psychiatric hospital, and I wouldn't have had a leg to stand on.

About a week into Florida Phase, I noticed three small, reddish sores on my arm. Everyone who lived down here in America's grundle told me going in that the mosquitos were nasty this time of year, so at first I thought they were just big bite marks. They went from aggravating to agonizing pretty quickly, but I didn't want to be a bitch about it and get kicked out of Ranger School. When you get an injury that is severe enough, they will medically recycle you (meaning that after you're done convalescing you have to start all over again) or just boot you out of Ranger School forever. If that happens, Ranger Regiment will most likely RFS you (relieve you for standards), which means you go down the road and turn in your hard-earned tan beret.

The next day, the three sores turned into ten. And not only were they getting bigger, but they were also starting to blister. They itched so bad, I don't even have a joke to describe the sensation. Every bit of mental energy I had been using to endure the challenges of Florida Phase and dream up ways of killing my tormentors, I now had to turn toward *not* scratching my sores—because if I did scratch them, they would pop. And unless you run an STD clinic in Gainesville, you never want to see the phrases "open sores" and "Florida swamp" in the same sentence. As much as I wanted to say something, I couldn't. Imagine trying to tell my instructors about my "condition" and asking them to give me a break until the itchy sores got better. That's how you get yourself taped to a palm tree with flypaper wearing nothing but a combat helmet with a Yankee Candle glued to the top. I just had to get through it and deal with the sores once Ranger School was over.

Eventually my skin got so bad that I couldn't wear my uniform in accordance with Army regulations. Every chance I had, I rolled up my sleeves or opened my blouse, looking for even the slightest bit of relief. At first I only did it in places I was sure no one could see me, but I quickly began to take greater and greater risks, starting with not giving a shit whether Trey Bullock saw me flouting the dress code.

From my very first day in the military, Trey had been one of my best friends. We went through OSUT, Airborne, and RASP together. We had just been deployed together, and now we were in the same platoon here in Ranger School—which never fucking happens. We were always competing against one another (we both wanted to graduate from Florida Phase at the top of our class), but we also always had each other's backs, no matter what, just like in the streets of Ramadi. When he saw how miserable I was standing in formation, he whispered over to me.

"Hey, man, are you all right?"

"No, man, you see these sores?" I opened my sleeves and showed him my arms. "I feel like I'm fucking dying."

"Jesus," he said, as a look of total horror crossed his face. That's when I knew how serious this was. I had seen that look before. It was the same look Detective Olivia Benson gets on *Law & Order: SVU* when a reluctant abuse victim finally gives in and shows her the bruises for the first time. *Something must be done!*

"I know," I said. "I don't know what to do."

"You better put your fucking sleeves down and figure it out when we get back, otherwise they're going to—"

"Ranger Best!" the instructor called out. "You trying to get a suntan?"

"Negative, Sergeant."

"Then why the fuck are your sleeves up?!!" He gave me a look like I'd just arrived to pick up his daughter for prom and handed her a corsage made out of NuvaRings. "GODDAMMIT, BEST, WHAT THE FUCK DO YOU THINK YOU'RE DOING? GET YOUR FUCKING BLOUSE SQUARED AWAY!"

"I can't right now. Look, Sergeant."

I walked over to him and politely showed him the oozing sores all over my arms. I've seen less recoil from three-and-a-half-inch turkey loads. He looked at me and shook his head violently.

"BEST, WHAT THE FUCK DO YOU THINK YOU'RE DOING WITH THOSE GODDAMN THINGS? GET THE FUCK AWAY FROM ME!"

"You betcha," I said under my breath. Part of me was happy that someone else finally got to see the shit I had been dealing with.

But most importantly, I took his fearful disgust as permission to go to Medical and get treated.

Getting medical treatment at an Army base during Ranger School is like going VIP to the Mayo Clinic if the Mayo Clinic used *actual* mayo to treat its patients. The "doctor" is typically a physician's assistant in training who has about 30 percent of what he needs—in terms of both knowledge and supplies—to treat the injuries he sees most often. My case was no different. Not only was the guy I went to a total dipshit, but if you questioned his diagnosis, he got downright offended.

"So, what do we have here today, Ranger Best?"

"You might want to stand back," I said, before taking off my shirt.

"JESUS FUCK! What is that?"

"Um, I was hoping you'd be able to tell me?"

This was not encouraging. When doctors in Florida are shocked to see something in or on your body and they don't know what it is immediately, you know it must be bad. After a long, hard look from a safe distance, he announced his diagnosis.

"I think those are spider bites."

"What? Spider bites? Are you fucking kidding me?"

"Are you questioning my medical opinion?"

"I am if you're trying to tell me that these wretched open sores are caused by spider bites. Come on, sir, this has to be something else."

"No. It isn't. It's spider bites, nothing more. I know you're probably not used to the conditions down here, but I can tell you straight away that those are most definitely spider bites."

"Fine," I said. I had no choice but to accept the confident verdict of my new friend Doctor Dumbass. "Give me something for the spider bites, and I'll be on my way."

At this point, I was willing to try anything he was willing to prescribe. You could have chopped up a Children's Chewable Tylenol and I would have snorted it off a rusty nail if it promised to relieve one second of my agony. What he gave me were some tiny spider bite pills and a bullshit topical powder that was probably just baby powder with a fancy arachnid label taped on the bottle.

Two useless hours after I got there, off I went in a short-sleeved T-shirt, certain of only one thing: I didn't have fucking spider bites. When I got back to the barracks, the rest of my platoon was getting their gear ready for another field exercise. It was the first time most of them had seen my sores, and they all looked at me like I was an extra on *The Walking Dead*. Trey walked over to me and sat down.

"Jesus, man, you all right?" he said

"No, I'm in a lot of fucking pain, and their diagnosis was just stellar."

"What did they say it was?"

"Spider bites. Can you believe that shit?"

As luck would have it, one of my buddies who was a 3/75 Ranger medic—I'll call him Jones—happened to walk by and overhear us. "Who the fuck told you those were spider bites?"

"The physician's assistant."

"Bullshit, spider bites," Jones said. "That's one of the most horrific cases of bullous impetigo I have ever seen. You better go back and see him before you lose a limb."

"I fucking knew it wasn't spider bites!" I said. "Motherfucker!"

If you don't know what bullous impetigo is, congratulate yourself and never, ever Google it. Let me give you the WebMD synopsis instead: Bullous impetigo creates a bunch of pus-filled sores all over your arms, legs, and back that start in the moist areas of your body (which, during Florida Phase, is *all* the areas of your body) and then burst open like grilled cherry tomatoes, only to scab over and leave scars roughly the size and shape of a car cigarette lighter. Still turned on? Keep reading!

The only way to limit the spread of the sores is to avoid scratching them or abrading them too much so they won't ulcerate prematurely. I managed to avoid scratching them, but there was nothing I could do about abrasion since my uniform was soaking wet twenty hours out of the day, effectively becoming a uniform-shaped kitchen sponge with the scrubby side facing inward.

"Hang on," Jones said. "Before you go back, I got something that will give you some immediate relief. I'm sure you're feeling some kind of hell right now."

"Spider bites hurt, ha." If I didn't laugh at the horror show dancing down my arms, I'd only be able to scream and rage.

He walked over to his bag, God bless him, and gave me a tube of steroid cream. The second I applied it, it felt like someone had just put a fire out on my skin. It was the most pain-free I had been since the first day I noticed the sores. I was so grateful to that observant, kind-hearted Ranger medic that I would have sucked his dick in front of everyone in that room. Balls too.

Feeling the medicine take hold, I started making my way back to Medical to find that physician's assistant and get this diagnosed correctly so I could heal properly. When I walked in to speak with him, I could already tell that my presence was unwelcome.

"Excuse me, sir, earlier you gave me the wrong diagnosis. You said I had spider bites and prescribed me medication for that—"

"What I diagnosed you with is exactly what you have," he said sternly.

"No, it isn't. I have bullous impetigo. It's not spider bites. I just need the proper prescription for that."

"Who the fuck told you that you have bullous impetigo?"

"One of my buddies is a Ranger medic, and he's seen this before. He also gave me this topical steroid cream to put on. It's really helping with the pain and swelling."

"So let me get this straight, someone else not only diagnosed you but gave you a non-prescribed medication that you used illegally?"

"I wouldn't say *illegally*. He's a medic, and he had some in his bag."

"Were you or were you not given prescribed medication that was not in your name, and did you or did you not use it?" he said, raising his voice.

"Yes, but he was only trying to help."

"What's his fucking name? I'm going to report him, too. He should fucking know better."

"I don't remember his name. He was just passing by."

"Bullshit. You just said he was your buddy. Give me his name."

"Again, I don't really know him. We're all kind of buddies out here, am I right?" I said, trying to defuse the situation.

"I ought to have you kicked out and medically discharged for something like this. Do you know how serious this is?"

"Sir, I just want to graduate and be done with this. I don't give a shit who made the right call here. What I'm trying to express to you is that I need your help. Can you please give me the correct prescription, sir? That's all I want."

After a couple minutes, the guy cooled off as I became more frustrated. I didn't want something so stupid as a misdiagnosis for spider bites in a goddamn swampland to end my military career. Of all the shit to get kicked out of Ranger Battalion for, this would have ranked right up there as one of the dumbest of all time. I can't even imagine what my brothers would have said.

Finally, the physician's assistant gave me a steroid booster shot in the ass, a shot of penicillin, and another tub of topical steroid cream and sent me on my way. I think he could genuinely see the pain in my eyes and how much I desperately just wanted to get better.

I also think he could see that if he got me booted out of Ranger School for this, I would have killed him.

Eventually, the treatment regimen did the trick, but not before 80 percent of the sores burst, leaving dozens of scars on my arms, back, and sides. Then, to add insult to injury, Trey ended up graduating Florida Phase as honor graduate and I got recycled back to the beginning of it. There is nothing more quintessentially Army than having to crawl back through the same shit swamps that infected you with the flesh-eating bacteria that was the reason you had to recycle in the first place.

And I wasn't even cured yet.

On what should have been my last day of Florida Phase, I stood in my "recycle formation" and watched as Trey, the ol' bestie, boarded the graduation bus to go make his family proud. I could feel Brehm's tab and scroll on the underside of my PC, pressing against my scalp, reinforcing in me the belief that I could get through this and reminding me not to be such a little pussy. Trey stopped on the first step of the bus and looked back at me.

"Hey, Mat?"

"Yeah?"

"I just wanted to say . . . tab check, bitch!" He laughed as he pointed to where his tab would soon be. It made me smile, because that's how best friends are supposed to treat each other. Don't you dare try to cheer me up, motherfucker. I expect you to kick me when I'm down, *like a man*!

By the time I finally graduated a few weeks later, I weighed 159 pounds, and my entire body was covered in bullous impetigo scars (my skin only got worse during the recycle phase). When my mom, who came to watch me get my tab, saw me for the first time, she gave me the full-on Olivia Benson. She didn't know whether to hug me or get angry and go on a crusade to figure out who did this to her baby. But she's a much stronger woman than I am, and she was confident that if I could survive Ranger School, I could also survive this.

"Just tell me you're okay," she said.

"I'm fine, Mom."

"Are you sure?"

"Yes," I said. And I was, more or less.

Until Florida Phase, I had such great skin that I could have been in one of those moisturizer commercials. Maybe it's Maybelline? Maybe it's genetics, motherfucker. Now I looked like the "before" picture in a Proactiv infomercial. I had to do something about it. So, like any rational twenty-year-old, I started getting large-format tattoos to cover up the scars. The day after my cousin—the full-bird colonel who'd magicked me into 2/75 like a boss—pinned my Ranger tab onto the left shoulder of my uniform sleeve, I set out to cover my actual left shoulder with a full tattoo sleeve.

I wanted something commemorative that combined imagery with script, something that looked cool but that was also personal and would remind me of this period in my life. I narrowed it down to two options and flipped a coin.

Heads, it would be an old-timey REWARD poster with the face of the physician's assistant that read: "Wanted in connection with being a fucking fuck face, fuck this guy."

Tails, it was a decorated memorial shield in honor of Brehm and Barraza.

It was tails.

Mom: "He's a boy, he'll grow out of it. Me: "This would be cooler if it had a laser on it."

"Even as a kid, I wanted to serve my country."—Every military book ever written. (It was laundry day.)

That's what brothers do, they play absolutely terrible emo/punk music together!

Shirts are dumb.

The only thing that reads
less than a Marine is camo
against maroon in low light.
Thanks, JC Penney portraits.

Seeing off my brothers (Alan on the left, Davis in the middle)
as they head to Kuwait for the Invasion of Iraq. Although
I thought only one of them was going.

My amazing mother and my former Ranger cousin shortly after pinning on my Ranger tab.

Captain Morgan got the idea from Sergeant Best. Change my mind.

Best. Tinder. Profile. Pic. EVER. Swipe righteous.

Trying to pull off the Zoolander blue steel in full kit.

Not getting shot always sets you up for a good smile.

Basic training.
Basic bitch.

Basic training is meant to bind you to your brothers.
MREs are meant to bind your bowels into a
balloon animal made out of poop.

Just a dude in the
middle of somewhere.

Screening of *Range 15,*
the zombie-apocalypse movie I made
with my friends and fellow veterans,
at Twentynine Palms.

More than mentors—a legacy we
should all live. Brothers
for life Dale Brehm (left) and
Ricardo Barraza (right).

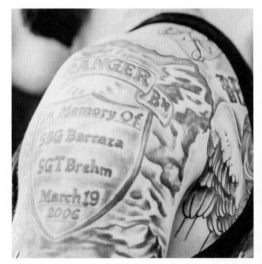

Respect.

Doing my best Stallone from *Cliffhanger* in the old Afghan.

From Ranger Battalion to being in business together, my man Rocco has always had my back.

Hey guys, check out my sweet beard while I contract!

Derek Weida and me shopping after skipping leg day.

Friends don't let friends
drink and fly. Just kidding,
I can't fly, but I can drink!

My beautiful mom and me
at the *Range 15* premiere.

Screening our movie in Iraq
with a bunch of badasses.

The military version of Lyft.

Filming videos with Rocco and Pilot X. God bless America.

Signing a whiskey bottle to a newborn baby was the least weird thing that happened at this Leadslingers Whiskey event.

Grill sergeant.

#freedomFRIDAY
GET SOME

Staying in shape after the military is SUPER challenging.

"It's okay to live a life most people don't understand."
—Fucking Pinterest quote

Little bird selfie.

Pretending to be an MMA fighter
with actual MMA fighter
Josh Tyler.

Best friends and
broken arms.
This is the garage
where it all started,
with Jarred Taylor
and Rocco in
El Paso, Texas.

Supporting one of my
Black Rifle Coffee
events.

I'd do Crossfit,
but mini-guns aren't
part of the WOD.

Cool guys don't look at explosions.

"No, that's my trailer,
Keith David, yours is over there.
And by the way, that uniform
is stolen valor."

On the set of *Range 15,*
goofing around.

Contractually obligated to put Ross Patterson in the book twice. And oh yeah, that's Marcus Luttrell and William Shatner too.

I really just put this in the book because I think it's adorable. Yes, I said adorable.

This should have been the book cover, but the publisher wanted to use something more "respectable" and "grown up" and "with less guns."

Chapter 8

Head and Shoulders
Above the Rest

After two deployments and eating a casino buffet worth of shit at Ranger School, I would have loved—and I mean *loved*—for my job as a warfighter in the 75th Ranger Regiment to begin and end with killing bad guys. Unfortunately, in war it doesn't work that way. There is always a lot more that goes into conducting operations than "Find bad guy, kill bad guy." There are systems and processes to follow, rules of engagement to obey, a lot of bosses to report to, and ATFATM (all those fucking acronyms to memorize). It's so bad the Army had to create field manuals— actual manuals, like for a car—to organize all the information. More than five hundred of them. I don't own five hundred of *anything.*

It was around this time that the military started to mainline Cialis and develop a raging hard-on for identifying every combatant we killed. They even created a log system into which they wanted us to integrate every EKIA (enemy killed in action). That meant once the action was over and all of our guys were accounted for, we had to stick around to make a yearbook out of these assholes: photographs, ID card, name and age (if we could find them), fingerprints, favorite color, senior quote, blah, blah, blah. I felt like saying, "Listen, Uncle Sam, I didn't go through RASP and Ranger School and get bullous impetigo to become a fucking data entry clerk. I do invasions, not inventory." At 4 A.M., after having successfully completed your objective, there is nothing more frustrating than having to go hunt down chunks of proof like a fucking truffle hog and then bring them back to be counted.

For a knuckle dragger like myself—even one who'd been promoted to sergeant and team leader—it was hard to accept that this information-gathering aspect of war was as important as pulling a trigger, especially when conducting direct action raids to kill or capture HVTs (high-value targets). But once you realize that you can't just *ask* someone who they are and where they hid the launch codes when all you can find of them is a limb (like with my old friend the none-armed man), you begin to understand the need for inventory and intelligence gathering.

The military calls this process "sensitive site exploitation" (SSE), and certain members of our unit were trained for it and were in charge of it. They documented the scene with video and searched the bodies for maps, documents, cell phones, computers, personal effects, and other bits of information that might be useful. They swabbed stuff and did hair and tissue analysis—all that *CSI* shit that I was too poor or too dumb to understand when I was growing up. Because war is war, and the Army is the Army, this theoretical system always went totally FUBAR in practice. A mission would blow up in your face, or it might go better than you expected, and then you'd be out there chilling with a bunch of bodies and either not enough supplies or no designated DNA analyst, because the mission planners hadn't thought you'd need one. If that happened, and you unexpectedly stumbled into a little game of *Guess Hussein?*, you were on your own.

Nobody I knew looked forward to this part of the job. The last thing anyone wanted was the delicate, precise tasks of SSE left to guys whose idea of a surgical strike was fucking as many VA nurses as possible when they were back home. Plus, the whole process got boring very quickly. You know that old proverb "Idle hands are the devil's workshop"? Well, *bored* hands must be the devil's whorehouse, because that's when things always got seriously fucked and someone ended up having to pay for it. Still, we knew this kind of exploitation and identification helped us going forward, so the general rule around SSE was "shut up and nut up." You never knew when you'd come across very sensitive information or information that might lead to a high-value target. It was like going on Terrorist Tinder and getting an immediate match— you didn't want to mess up that little love connection.

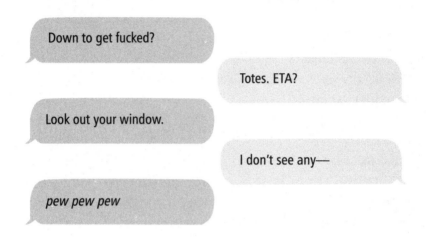

One night we got a call over the radio that ███████████ might have swiped right on some desolate road on the outskirts of Goatfuck, Iraq. My platoon had already done two direct-action raids that night. Nothing special, just the usual: kicking down doors, looking for bad guys who were already gone, getting shot at by their buddies who weren't. We were riding in the back of a pair of Chinooks, completely smoked on the way back to base, when the initial call came in: ██████ had just done a VI (vehicle interdiction) on an HVT. To most people, "vehicle interdiction" sounds like a fancy military phrase for "traffic stop," and in a sense it is, because it usually involves stopping a suspicious vehicle and either seizing its cargo or detaining its occupants, or both. In Iraq, however, VIs can go a little differently, especially when an HVT is involved. In a nutshell, we roll up on the skid of a helicopter, smile and wave at the asshole who hates Americans, and if he's one of the dudes who has been trying to blow up our people, we serve him with a good old-fashioned Grand Slam breakfast of 5.56 and 7.62.

It was 5:30 A.M.—typically the end of our workday—and all I was thinking about was getting back to base and knocking out a quick gym session before I went to bed. It was arm day. Those curls for the girls and tris for the guys weren't going to do themselves, after all. That's when my earpiece crackled alive for a second time. The ████ guys had just turned the HVT into a beard-covered s'more inside his late model Toyota Campfire, and they needed us to land and search the vehicle since they didn't have the manpower.

"Best," my squad leader says over the radio, "we need to go back out and ID the target."

Reluctantly, I press the mic button. "Roger. How far out are we?"

"Ten minutes out," he says.

Jesus titty-fucking Christ, doesn't anyone have any respect for arm day anymore!!?

By the time we land, dawn is approaching and the sky is starting to go from pitch black to that strange gray-blue color that normally means only one thing in special operations: Your ride is about to leave your ass there. The 160th SOAR is hands down the best aviation unit in the world, but these Chinook 47s are big, easy targets when they fly during the day and frankly, no one wants to play dodgeball with RPGs (rocket-propelled grenades) on their flight home, not the least of whom are the guys in the cockpit whose job it would be to dodge, dive, dip, duck, and dodge.

The helo pilots drop our team just beyond the torched vehicle and take off. I'm headed over to the car to make a quick assessment of the target when the platoon sergeant approaches me.

"Hey, Best, we got one guy charred up pretty bad. He's still inside the vehicle," he says before leaving to set a security perimeter with the rest of our platoon.

I pull my buddy Danny Fulton aside. Danny has outranked me since I met him on my first deployment to Mosul. He has been a badass far longer than that, in part because he is an early balder, and like any man who starts losing his hair before losing his virginity, he is pissed off at the world. He's the type of guy you wish you could parachute into Berkeley to knock some sense into all those entitled assholes who think that no war is justified and that all cupcakes grow on vegan rainbows. Combine that with professional training in the dark arts of not giving a fuck, then stuff it inside a six-foot-two, 220-pound frame, and what you have is a turducken of maximum pain and minimum sensitivity.

Obviously, Fulton is the perfect guy to handle the kind of identification surely awaiting us inside this charred vehicle.

"I'm thinking you and I should do this alone so the others don't have to see whatever the fuck it is we have to do in that car," I tell him.

"Roger," he says.

In this line of work, it's inevitable that you'll get your fair share of grotesque visuals. But if your team (like mine) has a lot of younger guys who haven't seen many dead bodies yet, or at least not dead bodies that promised to be as nasty as this one, you might as well ease them into it if you can. My opinion has always been, as a leader, the more shit you can put on your plate, the less of it your team has to eat.

Without a lot of fuss, Fulton and I quietly sneak over to the car. When we get there it dawns on me that we don't have any SSE kits on us to properly ID this body. No one in the platoon does. We used all of them on the dead guys from the target we left thirty minutes earlier. Quickly, we radio the ground force commander for some sort of guidance on the course of action they want us to follow. They respond with the kind of sympathy and understanding we've come to expect from military leadership.

"You need to get DNA off of that dude. I don't care how you do it. Figure it the fuck out."

"Roger," I say, shrugging to Fulton. He's keyed into the same channel, so he hears their response. "This is kind of a fucking ridiculous request, right?"

"It's the military, isn't it?" He laughs.

As we approach the car, I peer in through the window and finally get a good clean look at what we're dealing with. It's not the worst I've ever seen. The body's still identifiable—I mean, it's clearly a *person*—but anything more than that is going to take some work, because the dude looks like the top of a Texas brisket.

The first thing we have to do is get into the vehicle and cut this guy out. It's a simple task, but not an easy one. The fire hasn't just cooked the car's occupant, it also melted the car's door handle and locking mechanisms. It's going to take some elbow grease.

Once Fulton and I get the driver's-side door open, we each grab a limb and start to pull him out, but he won't come easy. Even in death, this motherfucker is resisting us. We do our best to keep the body intact, but inevitably some of his torched skin doesn't come with him. It's stuck to the leather seats.

Have you ever put cold meat on an extra-hot grill that you forgot to oil up beforehand? You know how it starts to scorch almost immediately, and then you try to flip it so it doesn't burn too badly on that side, but it's stuck to the grill and the only way to pry it loose is to scrape at it with the edge of your tongs? And then even if you are able to successfully turn the meat, when it's all said and done, the bit of flesh that was still stuck has become a layer of coal-black char that is practically fused to the grill grate and won't come off unless you get the grill ripping white hot and then use a coarse steel brush and scrub the shit out of it? His skin is stuck to the leather seats just like that.

All right, who's hungry!?

"Now what the fuck do we do?" Fulton says as we lay (most of) the driver on the ground away from the car. He's less Al-Qaeda, more al pastor, and neither of us quite knows how to dig into the problem.

"This is a new one for me, dude."

"How the fuck do they expect us to get DNA off of someone like this with no kits and burnt-ass fingers? This is so fucked."

"We're going to have to improvise," I say, looking down at my watch.

Whenever you're on a target, time is obviously of the essence. We tasked the rest of the team with securing the road in both directions, but you still never know how long it's going to take for other Al-Qaeda to ride up out of the desert to survey which one of their buddies just got bombed back to Paradise. Feeling the seconds tick away, I start flipping through my mental Rolodex of relevant skills.

People assume that since you've been through RASP and Ranger School and had all this military training, you must know everything there is to know about war. They think you're an encyclopedia of fucking shit up. Not to get all Liam Neeson on you, but the reality is that we're each trained with a very particular set of skills, and identifying dead burned-up people without any medical equipment is not one of the skills Fulton and I have. We're just two young Rangers, exhausted in the middle of the desert, with a char-broiled bad guy lying at our feet, trying to figure out how we get this asshole identified with enough time and energy left for the gym.

"We gotta get fingerprints and dental, right?" I say in the most confident voice I can. "That shit has DNA. Let's just get that."

"Great. How do we do that?" he says, looking at me like I know what I'm doing.

"I got a Leatherman," I say, as I pull out my knife.

"What, you want to pop his tooth off like a bottle cap?"

"I'm gonna rip it out with the pliers."

"C'mon," Fulton says, "you couldn't pull his needle dick out of his pants with those candy ass pliers."

"There's only one way to find out."

Fulton takes a second to look over the body again, as if he's Gil Grissom all of a sudden.

"Let's give it a go."

Fulton grabs the back of his head as I pry open his jaw with my left hand and spend a couple minutes digging around inside his mouth with my right hand, trying to carve out some teeth. I am going at his mouth from every conceivable angle, trying to find the point of maximum torque, but nothing is working. I heard once that dentists, as a profession, have the highest rate of suicide. I'm starting to understand why, because I'm really getting pissed off. I feel like I'm trying to weed a garden and I've run into a plant with a massive taproot connected to the other side of the earth. I'm only wasting time, and by now I'm flirting with the daylight.

Fulton was right. What I really need is an honest-to-goodness pair of pliers. I look up at him and ask, nearly out of breath, "You got any other ideas?"

"I was beginning to think this was a pretty solid plan, actually," Fulton says.

Staring down at this lifeless and burnt sack of shit as the sun is starting to come up, I can see only one viable alternative. "You want to just cut this fucker's head off? It'll probably be easier."

"Yeah, let's do it." Fulton responds immediately. He is all-in, no hesitation whatsoever. Man, I love that dude. He just doesn't give a shit when it comes to getting the job done.

"You want to hold the head?" he asks, like it's his bridal bouquet and I'm the maid of honor. Then he whips out his own Leatherman.

"Doesn't look like I really have a choice," I say. What I'm really thinking is: *Oh, so MY tool is too shitty for some teeth, but YOURS is somehow going to cut off a fucking head?*

I slowly tilt the Al Qaeda fighter's head back and Fulton starts cutting through his neck. I glance over the top of the car and see my platoon with confused looks on their faces, trying to figure out what we are doing. I can't imagine what it looks like to see us on our knees over a body; me holding perfectly steady as Fulton pumps back and forth as he saws. Oh wait, I *can* imagine how that looks—like we're Eiffel-Towering a corpse. When I look back down at the head, I remember thinking to myself how lucky those younger guys are that they're not seeing this. Any one of them could have very easily ended up with a lifetime of nightmares, and I wanted to protect them from that until they had kids with their first ex-wives, when the nightmares are real.

I try to learn something new every day. That day, I learned that it doesn't take that long to cut a head off. There really aren't any ligaments or hard structures in the neck, except for the spine, and even that's not very challenging. I've had a harder time getting the drumstick off a rotisserie chicken than Fulton did shelling this dude's bean. The whole thing took less than thirty seconds. For a couple of first-timers, this has to be some kind of record.

Once Fulton gets the head off, I place it in the garbage bag and we move on to prints. Our initial instinct is to cut off the guy's fingers. It's not like we need his palms—the VI team already read this shitbird his fucking fortune. Fulton makes a good point, though: Five fingers would take a lot of work, and the skin might come off the burnt ones if we're not careful.

"You want to just cut off his fucking arm?" he suggests.

"I think that would be most time-efficient," I reply, very aware, again, of how long we've been on the ground and the amount of light filling the sky.

"Then let's save fucking time. Grab his wrist."

"All right, give me a second," I say as I adjust and re-secure my black medical gloves. I might get PTSD from this horror show, but I'll be goddamned if I'm going to get Hepatitis C from it too.

I reach down and grab ahold of the man's arm so Fulton can begin the procedure. As I grip his wrist, his flesh peels back down his forearm toward the elbow, like a fruit roll-up.

"This is nasty," I say. Fulton is trying not to hear me.

"Holy Christ, put your fucking boot on his chest so the skin won't keep moving."

I pick the skin off my gloves and clap my hands clean.

"You got this," he says. Gee, thanks, coach.

I take a couple of deep breaths before standing and steadying my boot on his chest as I grab his wrist again. Fulton takes a knee and positions himself on the ground down by his shoulder and starts trying to cut surgically through the arm. Immediately, I see that he's having difficulty because the flesh is too loose. Although I have absolutely zero basis in fact or experience for this opinion, I fully expected the arm to come off as easily as the head. Unfortunately, the limb is fully cooked, which makes it much harder to get any purchase on the thing. I bend down to help him and literally start pulling meat off the bone.

As I start to twist the arm, Fulton moves down to the rotator cuff and begins scooping it out like he's carving out the inside of a pumpkin. After about two and a half of the longest minutes of my life, Fulton and I finally free the arm from its socket and it pops right off.

Sweating profusely and exhausted, I look up at Fulton. "What do you think? Anything else we need to grab?"

"We got the head, and the humerus bone, right? I think we're good."

"They didn't want footprints, did they?" At this point, this deep into the dissection, there is no way I am leaving without making sure we have everything we need. If Fulton says the SSE guys back at base might want toe jam, I am fully prepared to put on my Rex Ryan face and get all up in those feet.

"I don't think so," Fulton says.

"Okay. Let's get the fuck out of here."

With the head and arm now inside the trash bag, I sling it over my shoulder like I'm Johnny Appleseed and we head back. Our platoon stares at us as we walk around the side of the truck with the half-filled trash bag. I smile and wave to them.

"We got everything we need. Everyone get ready for exfil."

"How'd it go with that guy?" one of the privates asks.

"As far as Al-Qaeda go? He was head and shoulders above the rest." I fist-bump him for good measure. He's still a cherry and not a total fucking nutbag, so he just nods back the way you do when you don't want the other person to know that you have no idea what they are talking about.

I look over at Fulton and shake my head. *Kids these days.* A couple of privates are kneeling next to us. I reach over to one of the more timid ones and slap him on the knee, before placing the bag in his lap.

"Hey, could you hold this for the ride back?"

"Roger, Sergeant," he says, completely unaware of the fact—to this day, actually—that he rode home with a severed head and arm in a garbage bag. Instead, he gets to read about it here in great detail, along with the rest of the world. You're welcome, Sparkle Tits!

When we finally get back to base, it's nearing 7:30 A.M., which is really late for us. Fulton and I go down to drop off our haul at the SSE room where the privates have already begun to lay out on a table everything they retrieved from the target buildings during the raids we completed earlier in the night. Since it's so late, no one officially assigned to SSE is there to intake and catalog the stuff. Usually no one sweats it if you leave the more basic shit unattended until someone arrives to go through it, since you lock up the room once the last person leaves. But a garbage bag with a head and an arm in it is anything but basic. I hesitate to just drop it off.

"We can't just leave it here, *right*?" I say, looking over to Fulton for clarification, hoping that the one guy I know who gives fewer fucks than me will give me the thumbs-up.

"I don't know, man. I'm fucking tired and nobody is here."

"So is that a soft yes?"

"It's a 'Let's try and find someone, *then* say fuck it.'"

For the next ten minutes, we walk around the base trying to find someone to give it to. Anyone gullible enough to take a lumpy, unmarked garbage bag off our hands without asking too many questions. We do a full circuit, but no one is up yet, so we head back to the SSE room. It's still just us, approximately one-eighth of an enemy combatant, and an empty command center.

"Soooooo . . ." I begin, like I'm dropping off a first date and hoping she asks me inside.

"I'm not taking that fucking bag back to my room," Fulton says.

"Me neither. Merry fucking Christmas." I drop the garbage bag on the table and we walk out. Fulton gives me a nod goodbye as I shut the door behind us. Walking down the hallway, he turns and heads toward his bunk, and I continue on to the gym.

Who the fuck knocks out a quick gym sesh after a night like we just had? That's a good question. Although back then I probably would have said that's a stupid question because only a pussy skips a workout—especially bi and tri work—and this was just like any other day, NBD. The reality is that you've got to put your emotions somewhere when you have an experience like this. The thrill of war turns to the terror of war, if you don't get them out of you. I was lucky that I had music and working out, even if I didn't fully realize it at the time.

I don't give any of it another thought until I am awoken by a loud knock at my door. I look at my watch. It's 4 P.M. *What kind of stupid fucking asshole would wake me up this early?* I open the door to find my platoon sergeant standing there shaking his head, enraged.

"The XO wants to see you. *Now.*" He can barely get out the words, he's so livid. The XO (executive officer) is second in command at the company level. That means he has the power to fuck your life in half if he's not feeling particularly charitable that day.

I wipe the sleep out of my eyes and throw on my tan T-shirt and black shorts, before shuffling down the hall with Fulton trailing right behind me. We already know what's coming, and it's not going to be pleasant. The look of shock on my platoon sergeant's face says it all: We had crossed a line. Before we can even take a full step inside the ground force commander's office, the shitstorm makes landfall.

"Are you fucking kidding me?"

"What, sir?"

"Don't 'What, sir?' me! Did you guys cut off a goddamn head and arm?"

"Sir, you asked for DNA. You said you didn't care how we got it."

"I didn't ask you to drag half his fucking body in here and leave it on the table like a fucking bird dog!"

"Sorry, sir."

He gives us a long stern look, then nods. "It's handled. But don't you fucking guys ever do that shit again, you understand me?"

"Yes, sir," we reply.

The part of me that likes to drop bags of body parts into the laps of unsuspecting cherry privates wants to push his luck and ask his commanding officer what the proper protocol would have been, if bringing back the two-piece extra-crispy Al-Qaeda combo wasn't the right one. You can't ask a couple of sleep-deprived twenty-somethings to grab DNA without equipment or training and expect them to know what they're doing.

The part of me that likes killing bad guys without getting hassled about it just wants to go back to bed, though, so he shuts the other part of me up. When a commanding officer asks you for DNA, you give him more DNA than he can shake a beaker at. And if he gets a little testy about your methods, you respectfully shut the fuck up and then go on with your day. Because if you're being honest with yourself, while you *technically* gave him what he asked for, in reality you were being the worst Secret Santa ever. Just imagine the look on his face if *he* had actually been the one to open that bag, not knowing what was inside. It'd be like when you were a little kid and you'd open your lunchbox and instead of a bag of Doritos next to your sandwich, there'd be an apple or a banana or some other ridiculous nonsense—all because *someone* forgot to go to Costco that weekend.

A week later, a box full of the most tech-savvy James Bond–level DNA swab kits on the planet arrives. I'm talking high-speed swabs, some type of probing device, and all sorts of other shit that Fulton and I totally planned on misusing on future operational endeavors. To this day, I like to think that we had a little something to do with the advancement of field equipment in the military. I'm not saying they should erect a statue in our honor at Fort Lewis. A plaque would be nice. A *Jeopardy!* clue would be swell. Maybe a Lifetime biopic starring Seann William Scott as Mat Best and the guy who played Hank in *Breaking Bad* as Fulton? Ball's in your court, America.

I often wonder about the poor bastard who found the driver of that interdicted vehicle out in the desert—charred, decapitated, missing an arm. Imagine pulling up to a torched car sitting alone on a desolate road in the middle of nowhere, and here this fucker is, lying in the dirt, half the man he used to be. If you're that guy, mentally you're going to try to piece together what happened. That's what anyone would do. Our brains want to tell us a story about stuff like this, stuff about death. We want to order events and make sense of it all, to distract ourselves from the total randomness of life. There's no distracting this guy, though, because there's no story he could ever come up with that is even remotely sufficient to explain what he's looking at. Hopefully this account provides him with some clarity and some peace of mind.

Who are we kidding?

That illiterate motherfucker isn't reading shit!

Chapter 9

I Am the LAW

On one of my next deployments to Iraq, I was the platoon master breacher, which meant that I was in charge of all the things that go BOOM. The main advantage to this role was that I had the key to the platoon's ammo storage. At the base we were on, all the ammo was stored in a giant Conex box, which is basically a large metal shipping container. This thing was full of every fucking type of munitions you'd ever want. It looked like Arnold Schwarzenegger's weapons shed in *Commando*. We're talking ammunition of every caliber, frag grenades, every single type of breaching charge from explosive cutting tape to C4, det cord, all the best shit in the world and a surplus of it.

Under normal circumstances, you'd have to sign all this boom-boom out from the ammo NCO, who was a non-operational guy with the key and a tendency to be much less generous with the munitions rations than someone like me, who was out on target every night and believed that more was merrier. But since the tempo of this deployment was extremely high and we were running through lots and lots of ammo every night and I was the master breacher, I got the key instead.

In retrospect, that was probably a really bad idea, because by this point Danny Fulton (who had become my squad leader) and I had completely stopped giving a fuck. Over the course of these last couple deployments, our operational tempo had stayed high,

we'd survived plenty of close calls (like breaking down a barricaded door while an enemy combatant waited for me with an AK-
47 with a 100-round drum), and we'd been on more raids than
either of us could count. Fulton and I had each separately come to
the conclusion that we were going to die out there, so we started
pushing some serious boundaries on this stuff. If you're going to
die, why not have as much fun as possible and use as many weapons platforms as we could before our clock ran out?

One day, Fulton and I were in the Conex poking around looking
for cool shit to play with when Danny pulled out this Vietnam-era
upgraded rocket launcher called a thermobaric LAW (light anti-
armor weapon). Thermobaric weapons work like a hedge fund in
a hostile takeover—they suck all the oxygen out of the place and
then implode the whole fucking thing. The blast waves are ridiculous, and they leave a massive crater of destruction. Neither of us
had seen one of these rocket launchers outside of the movies, because by the end of the 1980s the Army had moved on to the Swed-
ish AT4, and the Ranger regiment started using the two-man M3
Carl Gustaf as their portable anti-tank weapons platform. We
hadn't seen either of those weapons in a while either, simply because the nature of the operational stuff we were doing on that
deployment didn't require them.

Around 7 that night, just after chow, Fulton walked into the
ready room looking for me. The ready room is the area in every
military unit where we stow our kits when we get back from a mission. Each person has a little cubby where they put their helmet,
their weapon, and their excess gear. (I sleep with my gun. So
should you.) The rest of the room is dedicated to everything else
we might need during an operation. As a team leader and the platoon master breacher, I spent a lot of time in the ready room
throughout the day, building demolitions or training up our privates on breaching tactics so that all of us were always on the
same page. Fulton knew this was where I would be this time of
night.

Without saying anything, Danny walked over to a locker, pulled the LAW out, walked over to where I was working, and put it down on the table in front of me.

"You're carrying this when we go out tonight," he said.

"Fuuuuck youuuu," I said, convinced he was joking around.

"No, you're carrying it."

"The fuck I am," I said.

"Do you want me to pull rank on you?" I love Danny Fulton to death, but seriously, fuck that guy right now.

"You really want me to carry a two-foot-long thermobaric launcher strapped to my back tonight?"

He really did. He advocated loudly that I take this ridiculous action hero rocket launcher on target, despite the fact that it would be super obnoxious when I was trying to kick down doors.

"Dude, when the fuck am I going to use this thing? We shoot people in the face with our guns. That's why we have CAS [close air support]. Why do I need this? I'm not in the anti-tank section."

Fulton didn't have an explanation that made sense to me. He knew damn well I was never going to shoot the fucking thing. I think he just wanted to fuck with me for a little bit. But he was squad leader, so unfortunately for me, he didn't need to have any other reason than that.

We started mission pre-briefing around 10 or 11 P.M., so by 8 I was in the ready room literally zip-tying this thing to my kit, getting more and more pissed with each tie I secured. When you add odd-shaped weight like this to a kit that you've learned how to balance perfectly, you just know it's going to dig into one of your shoulders more than the other or overburden one side of your back. When you're walking six or eight kilometers to a target, that has a way of making the whole experience pretty miserable. Even after setting it up as best I could, high on the center of my kit, it still ended up hitting the back of my helmet with every step I took, and that's some Chinese water torture shit, believe me.

When we got spun up for the night's mission, I split up from Fulton and led 1st Squad for infil with the 160th SOAR guys, landing about five kilometers out from the target building in the middle of some weird, shitty farmland surrounded by a network of irrigation canals. From looking at the maps and ground reference guide coming in, the whole place seemed like an un-navigable game of Tetris with one little dirt road down the middle that was basically a straight shot through the fields leading directly to the target. We tend to stay off the beaten path, but this road looked easy, a flat three-mile hike. More importantly, it had a running irrigation ditch on both sides that we could use as cover if we needed it.

As the squads came together, we pushed toward the target. The lead element was 3rd Squad, followed by 2nd Squad, and myself with 1st Squad following trail. Fulton and I, as our squad's leadership, found ourselves walking dead center down the middle of the road with our hands in our pockets just shooting the breeze— smoking and joking. Call it dumb if you will—if you won't I will— but we were in the middle of nowhere and we really didn't care. I especially didn't care, because all I could think about was this god-damn launcher strapped awkwardly to my back. I began quietly bitching to him about it.

"Jesus, this LAW is so fucking stupid."

"Best, you're kind of being a pussy right now."

"Dude, I am never going to shoot this thing."

Moments later, rounds start clacking off from the lead element. No one is particularly alarmed, since this was a nightly occurrence, but we all find cover down along the irrigation ditch. We're spread out over approximately fifty meters; across the road is a small village comprised of maybe fifteen buildings. Then it comes over the radio: "Troops in contact. 100 meters, 9 o'clock, multiple personnel." From my vantage point, I can see 3rd Squad taking fire, but I can't see exactly where it's coming from or what they're shooting at, so I start using the infrared laser on my weapon to paint sectors of fire for the guys in my squad to pull security.

"The front element is in contact," I tell a couple of the guys. "Make sure you guys are scanning those buildings because they'll probably use them as cover to try to flank us." The buildings are between seventy-five and one-hundred meters from where we lie.

With the advantage of knowing the landscape, it would not take long for a couple fighters to slip around us if we aren't vigilant.

As our guys begin scanning their sectors of fire, I try to orientate myself to see where we can maneuver to support the lead squad in contact. As I am scanning, an enemy combatant steps out from one of the buildings wielding an AK-47. Through my night vision goggles, I can see him about seventy-five meters away, looking left and then right, trying to figure out where we are. I can tell that he's really feeling himself like, "Yeah, the American infidels are going to die tonight!" But he has no clue where my squad is. His attention has been drawn to the gunfire he can hear immediately in front of him. I lift my infrared laser sight and paint a little infrared bindi of death right on his forehead. Then I pinged off two rounds that slapped him in the head and killed him instantly.

Shooting someone was nothing new to me at this point, but this time the milliseconds that passed between pulling the trigger and him hitting the dirt felt like they lasted a lifetime. In a way, I guess they did. Most times in war, things happen way too fast for anyone to really see anything or register human emotion. But in this specific instance, through my night vision goggles, I could see and feel the subtle nuances of his resolve, his motivation, and then his death. In a few milliseconds, I saw an entire lifetime. It was very Angel of Death-y. I had his life on a string, and the only question was "pull or don't pull?" It doesn't get much more immediate and primal than that.

After I killed the world's worst hide-and-seek player, my squad and I began engaging other combatants who'd maneuvered toward our position. Note to future terrorists: Don't try to gain a position of advantage on a Ranger fire team by running out in the open. It makes it really, really easy for us.

No, wait. Actually: *Please do that.*

In the midst of all this contact, the radio crackles and I hear, "Roger, first squad. Do you have a LAW?" I just start laughing. There is no fucking way that they just called for a LAW. I was surprised it even occurred to them that we might have one on target. We're such a precise light infantry unit, where clean mission execution is the order of the day, that the only way we'd have a LAW with us (and they'd know about it) is if the mission specifically called for something that could blow entire structures all to hell. Fulton looks at me and says, "Hey dude, they need the LAW up front." Is he still fucking with me about this? Did he bring 1st Squad in on it? Man, that dude really commits to a bit. As it turns out, the lead element was still in contact with a few combatants who had found cover in a building and were taking potshots at us. Along with launching some 40mm mortar rounds at the building, our guys figured while we're at it, why not also enforce the LAW? (Sorry, I had to.)

There was a weird moment of trepidation as Fulton ripped the LAW off the back of my kit and I prepared to cross the fifty-meter gap between our squads. I wasn't scared about getting shot at. What I was really worried about was screwing up. Fulton, like a dickhead, had ordered me at 7 P.M.—less than eight hours earlier—to bring this thing on the mission. At 8 P.M., I was tying it to my kit. The hour in between was all the time I had to learn how to operate it. I'd had the field manual out the whole time, walking through a couple test runs with a dud rocket we had in the Conex, but I had no idea if I could shoot the LAW accurately. I didn't even know if it still worked.

With AK rounds whizzing past my head and riffling into the dirt, I grab the LAW and start pushing toward the front element. As I'm running through farmland and getting caked with mud, I'm going over the field manual in my head. I remember thinking: *This is some serious John Rambo shit.* I didn't feel like I *was* Rambo; it was not that kind of visceral emotion. (That would come later.) It felt more like an out-of-body experience, as if I was in the audience at a theater watching everything go down on the big screen. Weirdly, I was having fun. No, actually, that's not true. I was having the time of my life and I didn't want it to end, until or unless it ended because *I* ended.

(In case you are wondering, I am available for children's birthday parties and middle school speaking engagements.)

By the time I made it to the front, 3rd Squad had figured out where the fire was coming from and they had it all lasered in for me. It was a first-floor bedroom window about 150 meters away. Since there was no infrared on this LAW because it was an antiquated piece of shit, I had to line up the shot through the sight aperture using my naked eye. I went through the motions one more time. *It's locked. It's cocked. The safety is off. It's pointed in the right direction. Okay, good to go.*

I got into position and took a good two-second breath. That exuberant feeling I had had thirty seconds earlier, sprinting across open farmland, was gone. In its place was a set of emotions that I assume would be very similar to whatever happens the moment before someone throws out the first pitch at a Major League baseball game. Deep in your soul, you want to whistle a strike right down the pipe that snaps in the catcher's mitt. But really, what you want even more is to *not* spike it into the dirt or throw it high and wide and hit the mascot. So to calm your nerves, you have to tell yourself that nobody's going to be aiming a radar gun at your fastball and to concentrate on getting it over the plate. That's all you have to do.

Fuck it, I thought, *I don't know if this thing is even going to shoot. I just hope it gets near that fucking window.*

"Back blast area clear?!" I shouted.

"Clear!"

With a recoilless rifle or rocket launcher, in this case the thermobaric LAW, you never jerk or anticipate recoil because there is really no kickback. Usually, it's the pause between trigger pull and launch that catches most people off guard. I pressed the button, held it steady, and waited for launch. *Inshallah, motherfuckers.* Two seconds later, the munition left the tube on a line and zeroed the window that the 3rd Squad guys had been painting for me. Just like the field manual described, that building went BOOM, right where I was aiming.

I stepped away from the launcher like I'd done it a thousand times before. No sweat. It wasn't a one-in-a-million shot by any means, but considering the circumstances it was better than bad. I think if you measured it on the scale of famous first pitches, with a 1 being Gary Dell'Abate at a Mets game in 2009 and a 10 being George W. Bush at Yankee Stadium after 9/11, I'd say I pretty much got the W.

After we cleared what remained of the building, we finished up all the fun stuff. You know, like sorting enemy KIAs and patching the wounds of dudes who had just tried to kill us. I was dying to talk shit right in Fulton's face about my shot placement, but I couldn't because I knew he'd have the perfect comeback: *I told you so*.

Chapter 10

Iraqi Rave Party

Not every day in Ranger Battalion is a shooting gallery at the carnival type of day. You forget that sometimes. You also forget that you tend to do things a little differently than the other branches of the military and that they look at you differently than you see yourself. Often you don't realize this until you get pulled from direct action raids and are attached to other units for short periods to complete specific objectives or to fill in when other elements of a unit are rotating home.

At one point in Iraq, I was tasked as the Ranger fire team leader along with four other Rangers to an Air Force Pararescue team (PJs) for a two-week CSAR (combat search and rescue) rotation. CSAR teams are typically first on the job any time an American helicopter or plane goes down. When we get the call, the Rangers secure and defend the crash site while the PJs do the recovery and provide any necessary medical care to the downed pilots and crew. Once they're good to go, the Rangers then plan the movement for exfil and return to base.

It's not uncommon to lose aerial assets during wartime, and this was especially true in the adverse conditions of hot, dusty Iraqi deserts and the 14,000-foot Hindu Kush mountains of Afghanistan. That said, it was rare enough that when it happened, it usually made the news back home. What that told me was, with only two weeks before I had to go back to my platoon for more direct action stuff, there was an excellent chance that this could be a nice, quiet little vacation.

Around 10 on the fourth night of my two weeks with the PJs, I was in our squad room, deep into a gnarly solo on the expert level of *Guitar Hero III: Legends of Rock*, when our radios kicked off:

"Roger, we have a downed fixed-wing."

So much for the vacation. An unmanned Predator drone had malfunctioned during takeoff and crashed about ten miles outside the wire of our base. Rushing to my kit room, my first thought was: *Dammit, I am NEVER going to beat "Through the Fire and Flames" this way!* Then I realized that I was getting all dressed up and I probably wouldn't even get to shoot anyone. That was even more disappointing. Pulling on all your body armor and strapping on your normal weapons load for a CSAR mission with no definable adversary is like putting on a condom to have sex with a blow-up doll. Sure, technically, it's action, but it's not like you're gonna catch anything . . .

Then the master breacher in me took over: *Wait . . . do I get to blow this thing up?* I'd breached plenty of doors and walls before, but never anything this big and complex. I had no idea how much demo I would need to get the job done. In uncertain moments like these, whether it's blowing up a drone or lighting up a party, I follow a very simple formula: *P* = Plenty. No one has ever said, "Damn, bro, you brought too much booze to the barbecue!" And I suspected that no one was going to complain that the crashed drone might get *too blown up*. Knowing that, I stuffed my backpack with ███████████ C4 plastic explosives, a few extra strands of timing fuse, and some command initiators . . . just in case.

Wheels up. Let's party.

We took off in two Black Hawks for the easy eight-minute flight to the crash site. As the birds dusted off back to base, we quickly secured the wreckage. I placed my team in a defensive posture around the site as the PJs worked to grab anything sensitive from the downed aircraft. PJs are like the world's greatest "Where's Waldo?" players. Give them even a little bit of time, and it won't matter where something is hidden, they're going to find that shit and grab it up. Everything was going smoothly when I heard the Air Force combat controller's radio frequency crackle. I stopped and took a knee next to him to see what was up.

"Roger, we are launching QRF [quick reaction force] immediately for backup," the person on the other side of the radio signal said.

"Yeah, we are all set here, guys," the combat controller calmly replied. "Stand by at gate, no need to launch, over." Combat controllers are experts in airfield seizure, air traffic control, air-to-ground comms, fire support, and all manner of command and control. When one of them tells you we're all set, we're all set.

"Negative," the voice responded. "We are en route to your position."

Jesus Henrietta Christ, who is running this donkey show? Because it clearly wasn't us—the guys with all the training and the guns and ████████████ brick of boom. At this point I was just wondering what kind of QRF they were sending. With how close and non-threatening our location was, I knew there was no way an infantry unit was on standby for this type of stuff. And it wasn't like ████████████ was fast-roping in for high-fives and photo ops any time soon. All I could do was patiently wait to find out. Then the radio crackled again.

"Roger . . . ummmm . . . what is your location? Our GPS isn't working." This was the Army, so it wasn't exactly a world-shaker that the piece of equipment designed to tell you which part of the soup sandwich you'd taken a bite of wasn't working. Still, it wasn't particularly reassuring that the *Quick* Reaction Force was this slow on the uptake.

The combat controller read out an exact ten-digit grid.

Silence.

"Do you copy, over?" the controller said.

Still nothing. Then I saw white Humvee lights far off in the distance breaking through a line of trees that bracketed our position for about four hundred meters on each side.

"DO YOU COPY, OVER!?"

The radio finally crackled to life again.

"I think . . . um . . . we are lost."

"Goddammit, these guys are more of a fucking hassle than this drone," I said, getting more frustrated. Not only were they making things complicated by distracting us from the task at hand, they were drawing attention to us by driving Miss Daisy with their white lights on.

"Ask them if they see my fucking IR laser," I told the combat controller. "I'll rope them into our position."

"Do you guys see an IR?" he said into his radio. "Four hundred meters, northeast of your position."

"Umm, negative, we don't have night vision."

Oh. What. The. Fuck.

That was it. I'd had enough of this shit. If I was going to die out here from something stupid, it was going to be *my* kind of stupid, not this nonsense. I asked the PJ to use his radio.

"Do you see a treeline in front of you?" I asked.

"Roger."

"Hit the treeline, then drive east."

Silence.

"TURN LEFT."

"Okay. Roger."

"When you break the treeline, take a right. Then look for Chem-Lights."

If you've never been in the military or to a nightclub in Las Vegas, ChemLights are those neon-colored sticks that you snap to activate and then they glow in the dark for twelve hours. When you see one at a club, it means "Look at me, I'm tripping balls." In this case, it meant "Look at me and please don't shoot."

I reached into my bag, pulled out a green ChemLight and a blue ChemLight, and cracked them. Since the guys didn't have night vision, I figured that this was the only way to get them to our position expeditiously. If walking out in the middle of the Iraqi desert like a fucking raver at Burning Man was what it was going to take for us to clear this target and get back to *Guitar Hero*, then that's what I was going to do.

"I will have a blue and green ChemLight. *Do not shoot me.*"

"Roger."

"Yeah, gonna need more on that one. What are you not going to do?"

"Shoot the guy with the ChemLights, sir."

"Exactly. Now hurry up."

The PJ and I made sure we had the same assault frequency on so that he could relay any relevant information coming from the Humvees, then I slung my gun behind my back and began sprinting the three-hundred-plus meters to the treeline. With the green and blue ChemLights in my hands, I looked like Tron just got caught fucking the neighbor's wife down the street. When I cleared the treeline, I saw the white lights of the Humvee convoy. There appeared to be four vehicles. I put the ChemLights up and waved them.

"Can they see me?" I asked the PJ.

"That's a negative."

You gotta be fist-fucking me.

"Tell them to look straight ahead!"

You'd think that waving a couple of shiny glowsticks in the pitch black of night out in the middle of nowhere would be enough to draw the eyes of a convoy full of trained American soldiers, but clearly it wasn't. So I started aggressively jumping up and down, doing Afghani jumping jacks basically (Google that shit), in the hopes that whatever ridiculous shapes my lights were making would grab their attention. Finally, their white lights flashed to signal that they had seen me.

As the Humvees sped toward me, my mind raced with possibilities: Which specific brand of stupid was I going to encounter behind the wheel of the lead vehicle? Whoever it was, I wanted to buttonhole them and remind them that I was a certified killing machine attached to a team of legitimate guardian angels, and if you get any one of us killed out of your own stupidity, that's effectively treason. It was so ridiculous, the thoughts going through my head. I felt like one of those old WWII veterans who lecture kids for being soft because they get rides to school instead of walking like they had to every day in the snow uphill both ways. I'm not going to pick on any specific units in the military because if you raised your hand to serve this country, well, you have my respect. With that said, it was obvious from this Keystone Kops routine that not *everyone* is meant to be "boots on the ground."

When the trucks finally pulled up, they contained a National Guard engineer unit full of poor bastards who looked like they had just been woken up from a good night's rest. If we had anything in common, it was that neither of us knew what to make of the other. I wondered how these chuckleheads ended up outside the wire in a situation well above their pay grade, while they wondered what all that cool stuff on my kit was. There was no time for foreplay, however, so I jumped on the side of the lead Humvee and directed them back to the crash area.

I placed the Guard unit in as best a defensive posture as I could with my Rangers, given that they had no night vision and kits that did not even come close to preparing them for being out here. It wasn't their fault. They were just following orders, probably from a commander who wanted to "see some action" before his tour was over. It was just lucky for them that I didn't have any more time to dwell on the shit show this could have become.

"We're ready to go. PJs got what we need. They said we can blow in place," the combat controller announced. Then he asked a question that was music to my ears. "Do you have any demo?"

Do I? I was like the Kool-Aid Man crashing through a wall: *Oh Yeeeeaaahh.*

Having never blown up a Predator drone before, now I was the one with a severe case of not knowing what the fuck I was doing. All I could be reasonably confident about was that if I looked really cool doing it, I would be fine. So I had my team push everyone back to the minimum safe distance, then I jumped back in there, yanked the C4 from my bag, rigged up ███████████ across the airframe (which was actually the appropriate amount of explosives to dispose of a huge-ass Predator) and wrapped all the large, reachable parts of the plane with det cords for good measure. Once I ran out of shit that goes boom, I hooked it up to one of the five-minute time fuses I brought with me and waited to finish off this Iraqi rave party in the way only the United States government was capable: with a multi-million-dollar fireworks show.

Burning . . .

The PJ team leader and I ran back to where we had pushed everyone, including the National Guard unit, in order to enjoy the—

BOOM!

The massive explosion kicked off and woke up the entire neighborhood. If anyone in this godforsaken place owned a car worth stealing, every alarm within a mile radius would have been going off. As for the drone . . . uh, what drone? That thing was vapor. Satisfied with our handiwork, we called in our ride home. Eight minutes later, two Black Hawks descended out of the darkness and scooped us up.

As the dust kicked off and covered the National Guard convoy we were leaving behind, I looked down to find the entire unit staring up at us in awe, like they were watching angels hop aboard death chariots for the ride back into hellfire. It was my first real glimpse at myself in someone else's mirror since going home for block leave after my first deployment. When you spend so much time training and living and fighting with one group of guys, you start to measure yourself only against them, not against the larger population back home or soldiers in the conventional units of the military. To this National Guard engineer unit, we were the epitome of the recruiting poster hanging in the storefront window next to their local Piggly Wiggly or tacked up in the high school hallway for Career Day when they were getting ready to graduate. We were the silent green-eyed killers who came and went under the cover of darkness, and they'd actually caught a glimpse of us in the flesh. We'd gone from *Guitar Hero* to superhero in the space of a couple hours, which was a pretty cool feeling, though I personally reject that hero label, since I could never beat that fucking game no matter how hard I tried.

Chapter 11

Balad. James Balad.

The way the cliché goes, senior year in high school is sup-
posed to be the best year of your life. You've got your solid group
of friends that you've grown up with over the previous three years.
You've got everything dialed in, and you know how shit works.
You know all the tricks and the shortcuts—what matters and what
doesn't. You're captain of this or that team, you have privileges
that the younger kids don't even understand. You basically run the
school, and the administrators stay out of your way as long as you
don't blow up too many things or get too many people pregnant.

Minus the restriction on blowing things up—breachers gotta
breach—that's what it was like during my fifth deployment as a
Ranger. I was coming into the final year of my enlistment contract. I'd made E-5 (Sergeant) on the previous trip. All my buddies
were either team leaders or squad leaders. And best of all, unlike
high school, I didn't *have* to graduate if I didn't want to. This deployment could be a victory lap of sorts, or I could run it back and
do another four years with a few signatures on a set of reenlistment papers. Coming into this fifth deployment, I was leaning
toward the latter.

Intentionally or not, the Army made that decision very difficult
when they sent us to Balad, Iraq, in June of 2008. The operational
tempo on this deployment was similar to previous trips, and we

were getting into TICs (troops in contact) nearly every night. Rarely would we hit a dry hole. And since this was late summer into early fall, there were no cold weather quitters, either. There were only fighters. As a result, we had most of the base's aerial assets at our disposal, and we did the majority of our missions as HAFs (helicopter assault force), serious *Apocalypse Now* "Ride of the Valkyries" kind of shit.

The whole thing was like a gift from the war gods. All that romanticizing of war that Fulton and I had been flirting with in our first couple years had steadily grown into a full-on love affair, and we were super excited to get our fuck on. When it came to combat, Fulton and I saw eye to eye on everything. Cutting off a guy's head will do that to a relationship, but I also think that in the two years since Brehm and Barraza had gotten killed, a lot of their leadership lessons had encoded themselves into our DNA. Those guys were always first through the door because their number-one mission was to make sure their teams made it home to their families. If anyone was going to get shot breaching a door or clearing a building, it should be them. That's how they saw it. Fulton and I didn't really talk about it directly, but we had an unspoken understanding on this trip that we would be the first through the door, and while we didn't want to get shot, if we did . . . well . . . so be it. We just wanted to kill as many bad dudes as we could and make sure that our men got home.

When you come to that kind of understanding, with a brother or just with yourself, it is one of the most freeing sensations you will ever have in your life. I felt ten times lighter, a hundred times faster, a thousand times stronger. At the time I thought this state of mind was unique to the war experience, and it made me want to live each day, each mission, over and over again for as long as I could. Like an endless summer. It wasn't until much later that I realized that you can have this feeling, or something pretty close to it, outside of war too. You can have it in art and in relationships and in business. All it takes is giving yourself permission to take risks and allowing yourself the freedom to fail.

rt of what made this epiphany so potent was that Balad was the best base I'd been stationed at since joining the Army. I had my own pod (private living quarters are something special in the military). There was a fucking pool, with sweet chaise lounge chairs. Imagine going to summer camp and while you were gone some rich kid moved into the neighborhood and his dad built a brand-new skate park and hired Tony Hawk to give free lessons every day. It was like that.

And the food options, sweethomealabama, they were glorious: Peet's Coffee, Cinnabon, Taco Bell. Because the majority of my deployments were spent on forward operating bases, I was used to living out of a rucksack and eating MREs (meals ready to eat) and shit chow that bound you up like geisha feet. Peet's and Taco Bell weren't just delicious, they set the clock to my morning and evening shits. I'd never felt so regular in my entire life. I never understood why people got enemas or colonics, but if they make you feel anything like my first week at Balad, well then, consider me converted.

Walking onto the base in Balad really was like moving into an episode of *MTV Cribs*. There are two ways to respond to this kind of abundance after experiencing such scarcity: You can slowly savor it, appreciating every bite, or you can gorge yourself on it until you want to throw up so you can make room in your stomach for more.

I wasn't sure which type I would be until one day, chilling in the pool, I decided to swim up to one of the hottest girls I'd ever seen OCONUS (outside the Continental United States) and say hello. This girl was not just "deployment hot." I'm talking real-life, on the streets of New York hot. She was the Wendy Peffercorn of the pool, and she was there every day.

"Hi, I'm Mat—"

"Are you Black Ops?" Wendy said in a stern but intrigued voice.

Oh, Wendy. You know the answer to that question. And you know that I know that you know.

When you're deployed and strolling around a big base like Balad, the service branches are distinguished by the different colors of the shirts and shorts people wear. The Army has gray T-shirts and shorts that say, you guessed it, "Army." The Air Force, which, judging by the revolving door of its uniform styles, is sponsored by Benjamin Moore, has whatever color pattern they picked that day that says "Air Force."

Special Operations units really try to not stand out. We wear black PT shorts, tan T-shirts with no insignia, beards, tattoos, and 5 percent body fat. We blend right in.

Wendy, this beautiful, wonderful young woman, knew exactly who and what I was. It's long been understood that Special Operations carry a certain allure. Overseas, the women knew it too. They knew you were most likely the guys out there killing Terry Taliban at night in defense of the American way of life and then coming back to base and waking up the next day like nothing ever happened. You were seeing and doing real war—the kind people tell stories and make movies about. A lot of people *wanted* to know those stories so that they could brag to all their friends once they got home. I'd even venture to say that some of them *needed* those stories. Sleeping with you was almost like sleeping with the cover of a romance novel:

> *There was still blood on his shirt, and he had this steely look in his eyes like there was something he wanted to tell me, but couldn't. In that moment, I had never felt so vulnerable in my life. I wanted to comfort him, nurture him, and be the woman he was missing in this world. . . .*

By asking if I was "Black Ops"—a term no one inside the military even uses unless they're fucking around—Wendy let me know that she was looking for the Special Operations deployment fantasy. She didn't have to say another word. I was happy to oblige. Still, I had to play it cool if I was going to lock this down, because I had my entire platoon staring at me from across the pool, waiting for me to fail so they could dive in and take their own run at her. If I chunked it and she got out of the pool, I might not get a second chance.

That's when the mortar alarms went off. Mortar alarms are a base-wide radar system that is supposed to alert you to incoming mortars that have a likelihood of hitting inside the base. Half the time the thing malfunctions and goes off at random, but everyone still has to follow protocol, which in this case meant getting out of the pool and taking cover in a secure location or getting down in the prone position.

"That fucking mortar better hit if it's going to cockblock me," I muttered to myself as I lay prone on the pool deck. Getting up off your face and collecting yourself to continue hitting on the hottest girl on base is not the easiest transition in the world. I had a lot of life experience, but I was still twenty-two years old and that kind of smoothness requires some red-belt-level rap.

"All clear!" someone shouted.

Of course.

I don't remember what I said after I dusted myself off and re-engaged with Wendy, but I managed to get her email address and charm her with my emoji game. A few days later, I "borrowed" a Hilux truck from the motor pool and we had our first date outside of a broken-down Iraqi Taco Bell. I had the pink taco platter. She had the Best burrito supreme. If that isn't love, I don't know what is. Pretty much every day from that point forward, I would go to the pool with her, we'd "fifty shades of grey" all afternoon, then I'd go get chow and prep to leave for our mission that night.

It was incredible.

In retrospect, I recognize that I was living a fantasy as a tattooed, douchier version of a real James Bond. *The name's Balad. James Balad.* At the time, though, I felt far more like I was walking in the footsteps of John Rambo: a man who lived for war and had nothing left to lose.

The *Rambo* movies were my favorites growing up, even before I knew I wanted to join the military. Here was this guy, played by Sylvester Stallone, who was the ultimate badass. He never died. Hell, he never even got shot. But he lived with this constant mental anguish that forced him to keep going, to keep moving forward, because war was all he had left. It was Rambo versus the world. Kill or be killed. That was his mentality, and that's what I loved about him. That's what I wanted to be. By the middle of this fifth deployment, I felt closer to that feeling than I ever had before.

I never told anyone on my team about this, because honestly, it was super lame. Who says shit like that? The answer is no one, which is why I didn't say it out loud, even as I was thinking it every second of every night we were out on target. The more intense a situation got, the deeper I went into the weirder parts of my brain. I would literally think to myself on missions at night, "I am Rambo. Good luck trying to kill me, motherfucker, because I don't give a fuck."

Don't misunderstand: I wasn't suicidal. Thinking you're going to die and wanting to die are totally different things. I didn't have a death wish. It's just that, in my experience, the more you deploy and face the dark realities that exist in life, the more comfortable you become with the idea of death. Sometimes you don't really care if it's you or the people you are hunting who die, just as long as it isn't the people you are leading. It's hard to explain to people who have never served in this capacity. I just loved what I was doing so much, especially on this deployment, that there was nothing anyone could do—least of all some piece of shit terrorist—to get in the way of me doing it. I mean, think about it: I'd wake up at 6 P.M., show people how to build crazy charges to blow up buildings, then I'd go practice raids, eat some Cinnabon, and get a beeper page to go out in the middle of the night to shoot guys in the face before rolling home to bang one of the hottest blondes I've ever had the pleasure of sharing a bed with. And the next day, I would go right back after it again. *I was fighting, feasting, and fucking*. EVERY DAY. That is wired into the male genetic code, and I was peaking out at all levels, all deployment, in a way that I knew would stick with me wherever I went in life, however long that life might last. And the more I did it all, the more I wanted—the more I *needed*—to keep doing it.

That's easier said than done, though, because ultimately, you are playing a very dangerous game, one where the key to winning is figuring out just how long you can play it while still having fun. And make no mistake: Killing bad guys is fun. Some guys get really good at the game, but then they get sick of it and bow out. Either mentally they're over it, or physically they just check out. For me, the fun never really seemed to stop, but I did start to realize that there were other kinds of fun out there and that maybe they were healthier than the kind I was having.

Between my fourth and fifth deployments in early 2008, I'd finally joined the social media revolution and gotten a MySpace page. I didn't think much of it at first; it was just a way to stay in touch with my brothers and some of my friends from high school. In Balad, I checked it every week or so to read and respond to messages. Checking it weekly instead of daily ended up being torture, because rather than seeing the trickle of daily life events, I'd see this massive accumulation of carefree fucking around from everyone in my Top 8 that made it seem like their entire existence was one long weekend. I'd be scrolling through photos of house parties and beach bonfires—everything normal twenty-two-year-olds do—and then head over to the ready room to put together charges for that night's mission, which might be some piece of shit mud brick building full of bearded assholes who wipe their asses with their bare hands. The cognitive divide was massive, and it started really playing with my head.

What I was looking at, I realize now, was the other half of that cliché about the senior year of high school I talked about earlier. At some point, you bump into guys who graduated a year or two ahead of you and they let you in on a little secret: There's more after high school, and it's way better. Dominating high school is cool and all, but college? Working for yourself? Not having to do anything if you want to be a bum for a while? That's real. That's freedom. And it's fucking awesome.

MySpace put a mirror in my face and forced me to look into it, and what I found was someone whose decisions had taken one hell of a mental and physical toll, no matter how much he wanted to deny it.

Then another question crept into my head: Would I ever be able to transition back into the real world and assimilate? It seemed to me that going from hunting humans with lasers to hunting for a "normal job" in the private sector would be virtually impossible. The idea of going on a civilian job interview was weirdly terrifying:

> **Interviewer:** Do you have any management experience?
> **Mat:** I was a team leader.
> **Interviewer:** Great. Tell me, how did you normally handle conflict?
> **Mat:** Usually a short-barrel M4 carbine. But sometimes, also helicopters.
> **Interviewer:** Thanks . . . We'll be in touch.

This was more than a passing concern for me, because the deadline for reenlistment was coming up fast. Until very recently, my mind had been set. I was going to sign those papers and keep doing what we were doing: living the dream. But suddenly the decision wasn't so clear anymore. With only two days left to decide, a message popped up from one of my best friends back home who knew that my deployment was about to end.

> Hey Mat, when you get back, why don't you come live with us? We're moving to Los Angeles, there's like three of us who are going in on renting a house together. We're going to fuck shit up. Miss you bro, we'd love to have you.

I remember sitting there, staring at the screen, unsure how to respond. After careful thought I typed back:

> What are you guys going to do for jobs?

I checked my messages the next day and found this response:

> What are you, a fucking dad? Dude, we're 22. Who gives a shit? We're
> going to party and fuck hot chicks all summer. We'll figure it out when
> we get there. You in? Need to know soon so we can fill in your room if
> you don't want to come.

The words "What are you, a fucking dad?" stung me, because it was true. Damn. Why did I care what they were doing for jobs? Forget about assimilating into the workforce, could I even be a normal kid and have fun again? Had I seen too much to live the life of a typical twenty-two-year-old? If his offer sounded appealing to me—and it did—my only concern should have been partying and hooking up all summer, not how we were going to keep the lights on while we did it. Was I going to age too rapidly and burn myself out over here and miss all of my twenties if I stayed? Probably. Would it be more rewarding to stay? Maybe. Would I regret not giving the carefree twenties a shot? I didn't know.

After a grueling mental back and forth over the next forty-eight hours, I decided not to reenlist. After chasing my military dreams since I was sixteen years old, after fighting for my country through five deployments, through many narrow misses and several tragic deaths, I decided to go home and try to be a kid again. I quit war cold turkey. For now at least. . . .

Chapter 12

Snowflakes in Los Angeles?

The day I got out of the Army, September 13, 2008, I stood there and watched as my platoon headed out on a training exercise. For four years, I'd joined them on exercises just like this, to places just like where they were going. It was old hat. No big deal. They didn't do anything differently than they always did; it was me who was different. These men were readying themselves for the next deployment cycle, right as the conflict in Iraq was turning into a total slaughterhouse. I, on the other hand, was preparing to get in a cab and go to the airport, where I would hop on a plane and get shitfaced with Southwest drink coupons.

It was not an easy pill to swallow.

Still, the first couple months back in Southern California were great. Finally, I was living that MySpace feed. My friends and I partied, went to the beach, drank, and chased girls, just like we talked about. I had no one telling me what to do or where I had to be. I'd wake up at 0500 out of habit, look at my phone, realize I could sleep until 1700 if I wanted, then faceplant back into my pillow or the girl lying next to me—whichever was softer. I was a free man. A total fucking bum. You'd think the freshness and the newness of all that would be liberating, and for a while it was, but eventually I came to realize that there wasn't actually anything fresh and new about it at all. Going home and getting annihilated every night was what I did after every deployment. The only thing that was remotely different about doing it in L.A. was the *type* of people I was doing it with.

The stereotype about L.A. people is that they're all plastic, superficial phonies. Those people certainly exist in L.A., like they do in any big cosmopolitan city, but in my experience the young L.A. people I met out at restaurants and bars those first couple months were all genuinely, authentically . . . *awful.* My buddies and I would go out every night, we'd end up in conversations with different groups of people, and then, when they found out I was a veteran who'd just returned from Iraq, it was T-Minus Cocktails before one of them found a way to insult me without even realizing it. This was right around the 2008 presidential election, too, when *The Daily Show* was at its most popular, so everyone was now a foreign policy expert.

"Uggh, George Bush, I swear to *Gawwd.*"

"Yeah but he's not running ag—"

"This fucking oil war . . . it's *sooo* gross."

"Well, it's a little more complic—"

"And Halliburton, right? Dick Cheney shot someone in the face!"

Then they'd all laugh at their funny joke and basically wait for me to explain myself. What I wanted to explain was how easy it would be to kill all of them before any of them could reach the front door. Instead I took the mature route and engaged with their ideas, to the extent they had any. I talked to them about my experience. I explained the military family I came from and described the brotherhood that made all the hard work and sacrifice worth it. I talked as little about politics or policy as I could because, really, what did I know? I was the sharp end of the spear, not the guy aiming it. Most people, to their credit, were receptive to what I had to say and appreciated my perspective, but because they were also just so fucking stupid, the way they expressed their appreciation was where the insults happened.

"That's really interesting, I never thought of it like that. You know, when you first said you were in Iraq . . . you're totally not as brainwashed as I thought you'd be."

"Brainwashed"?

Bitch, I will—

Deep breaths, Mat. Deeeeeeeep breaths.

I didn't go out to get judged and psychoanalyzed by people like *them*. I went out to get drunk and laid . . . by people like them. This made me want to skip all aspects of conversation and just get right to the drunken sex part.

Ultimately, I couldn't be too mad at these kids—and believe me, they were kids—because theirs was not the kind of stupidity that was learned. It was the kind that was baked in. Someone *raised* them to be this shitty. It'd be like Siegfried getting mad at the tiger when it nearly bit Roy's head off. How could he? They were fucking with a tiger! Still, after enough trips around the carousel of ignorance, I decided to hop off and stay home more often. Jameson is cheaper when you buy it at Costco anyway, and playing video games is way more fun than listening to idiots, especially since you can turn off a video game whenever you want. Plus, within a couple of months I'd moved in with a girlfriend, which pretty much meant live-action insta-porn any time we wanted it.

It wasn't long before I realized I was running out of money, however. I woke up one morning, went to the ATM to get some cash, looked at my bank balance, and noticed I had less than what I needed for next month's rent. It only took four months of drinking in L.A. to burn through what little I was able to save from my pittance of a military salary. I had to do something, not just for my savings but for my sanity as well.

So I went to college.

That's what you're supposed to do, right? Serve your country, then use the GI Bill to get a free education. Be all you can be, then learn all you can learn. I felt fully capable of attending school and getting a degree. While I wouldn't say that I was a consciously purpose-focused person at this point in my life (I had no idea what I should major in, for instance), I was certainly mission-focused, so if I approached studying and the course load from that perspective, I knew I'd be okay. Hell, half your job in the military is to sit there and listen to someone lecture you, so I was already 50 percent good to go.

I decided to check out California State University, Northridge ("Cal State Northridge," for all you diehard Californians out there). It was close to home, I got in-state tuition, and their mascot was Matty the Matador. How could you not go to a cheap school where the mascot is named after you? Even if he is a bull-dodging foreigner in a stupid fucking hat.

My first day on campus was filled with a mix of emotions. There was the typical bout of nerves that comes with having a new experience and being in a new place. There was some excitement at the opportunity for a new beginning. But there was also a healthy amount of fear that, much like the people I met out at the bars in L.A., I would come to absolutely hate everyone and they would hate me right back. It was a reasonable fear. I was older than most everybody who would be in my classes. I was covered in tattoos, which wasn't the norm back then. And I'd just gotten done fighting a war that pretty much every young person around me loathed and cited as one of the reasons they had voted for Barack Obama, who had just been elected.

My first stop before pulling the trigger on enrollment was the veterans' affairs counselor in the registrar's office. A lot of big state schools have one of these people nowadays. It's a really great service. They help you get your GI Bill paperwork squared away. They help you transfer over credits from any relevant courses you took while you were enlisted. And they help you map out course selection based on what you want to study, even if, like me, you didn't really know yet. They also give you what amounts to an informal orientation.

"Mat, we're so excited that you are thinking about pursuing a degree here with us," the counselor told me. "We try really hard to make our veteran-students comfortable in this different kind of learning environment, because we know how hard this transition can be for some people."

Do you, now?

"It's funny. Some of our veterans and our younger students have a lot in common. In many instances, they struggle with the lack of structured days in the same ways."

The same? Oh, I doubt that.

I understood what the counselor was trying to say, but the way she was couching things made me start to wonder if my initial fears were well founded. Was this place going to be full of intellectual enemy combatants? When our meeting ended, I walked out and headed for my truck, which was parked way on the other side of the campus where I didn't have to pay for parking. I was nearly broke and I am a natural cheapskate anyway, so I wasn't about to give these people my money if I didn't have to. I also figured having to walk across the large urban campus would give me a chance to take the measure of the place.

It met all of my expectations, and not in a good way.

The random snippets of conversation I overheard as I made my way out of the administration building were completely disconnected from any reality that I recognized. The young men and women whose words I was registering as I walked certainly weren't ready for the real world that I knew, from experience, was getting ready to knock at their door and detonate in their faces. It takes everyone a little time to figure "it" out. I get it. But the fundamental lack of understanding of how the world works, the lack of awareness of how privileged they were, and the absence of basic respect for America that I heard coming out of the mouths of these kids was like listening to a sixty-minute loop of nails on a chalkboard. If these conversations were representative of the dialogue I would have to entertain while enrolled here, they were about as likely to survive in the real world as I was to survive on this campus.

I kept moving. I walked through this little park area called Orange Grove and past the campus duck pond, and I quickly realized that a disproportionate amount of my attention was occupied by worrying about some of these dipshits walking too close to the water's edge. I honestly thought they might fall in and sink like the box of rocks they were. I was only twenty-three years old, the same age as many of the seniors and first-year graduate students at the school, yet I felt like I was their babysitter. Even a cursory evaluation of the students' orientation to their environment revealed a general obliviousness that, in the real world, would have real consequences.

But that was just it. I wasn't in the real world. I was on a college campus. My immediate concern for these kids was completely unwarranted. No one whose path I had crossed so far that afternoon had actually done anything to arouse real concern. And why would it? They all lived in a giant bubble. They'd experienced no danger, no risk, no decisions involving life-or-death stakes. And the entire system was set up to keep it that way for as long as possible. College wasn't their proving ground. It was their playground, with no sharp edges and no one keeping score. Emotionally, they were lumps of Play-Doh drowning in Purell. Practically, they weren't even that useful.

I stopped in the cafeteria to grab a bite before heading home. One of the students standing by the rack of trays noticed my tattoos and my lack of a backpack and asked me if I could go get someone to bring more trays out, like I was the janitor or a cafeteria worker or something. *Do I look like a janitor, motherfucker? Wait, don't answer that.*

I ate my lunch in silence and absorbed more of the conversations going on around me. It felt like a giant dye pack full of stupid had just exploded inside a bag of stolen money (their tuition, maybe) and covered me in the residue. It was more frightening than anything I'd heard out in the open air of campus. It was as if their unlimited meal plan somehow made the cafeteria their safe space: *If I can* eat *any amount of this ridiculous shit I want, I can* say *any amount of ridiculous shit I want too.*

Witnessing all this, I had a choice: I could rage at them for being such thoughtless, clueless, careless, gutless, spoiled garbage people, or I could get up, throw away the rest of my lunch, quietly walk out, and never come back.

The correct choice is pretty obvious, but it wasn't easy. There was real, actual rage flaring up inside me. It had started to come out more and more in recent weeks at bars my friends and I would go to. I would drink aggressively. I would *spend* aggressively. Recklessly. I made fuck all in salary while I was in the Army, that is true, but the real reason I went through my savings so fast was that I drank most of it and pissed the rest away. I'd wake up really mad—mostly at myself but also at the people around me. People like these shitty college kids. Actually, no, it's not totally their fault: people like their *parents*. I would get so mad at the parents that I wanted to punch their kids right back up into their urethras and undo their births.

That's normal, right?

As I drove home from Northridge, all I kept thinking was, "Okay, Mat, you have to stay active if you're going to make this transition. You have to keep moving." It was not unlike my time in the service. If you want to clear through the objective, you've got to keep pushing forward. If you stand still, you're a sitting duck. If you go back, you just make it easier for whatever is chasing you to catch up. But how do you push forward in this scenario? Push forward to what? What is there that is even remotely stimulating? With college out the window for now, what was I going to do?

The obvious next choice was to become a PMC (private military contractor). It is the immediate next step for a lot of special operations guys when they get out. Two of my Ranger buddies, Trey and Josh, who got out around the same time I did, went straight into contracting. The agencies love to grab up guys like them as early as they can, because their ideal candidate still has his security clearances and an up-to-date understanding of the area of operations he's likely to be working in. The smoothness of that transition from public to semi-private work is very enticing for most special operations guys who do it, and for those who are less enticed, the fact that contracting pays a fuck-ton of money helps bridge the enthusiasm gap. How could it not—you're doing a similar job in support of the same cause, but now you get to wear civilian clothes, eat way better food, and make three times as much money as you did before. It's kind of a dream gig.

I wasn't interested. I mean, *I was*, but at the same time I also wasn't. When I left the Army, I was certain that I could go back to civilian life and be a normal twenty-three-year-old. I could slide right into the flow of normal daily life and go with it like everyone else out there who hadn't gone through the kind of shit my buddies and I had in combat. And I stubbornly still felt like that was true, even if the drinking and the spending and the rage argued to the contrary. It was L.A. that was the issue, not me. It was entitled college kids with stupid ideas who were the problem. I knew what time it was, if you know what I mean.

The next day I went to the one place that every young, impressionable, know-it-all college dropout turned to in the mid-2000s when they were looking for a temporary solution to a much longer-term problem: Craigslist. I spent hours scouring the site for any kind of job that seemed exciting, and I learned a valuable lesson in the process: Casual Encounters is not where you look for easy one-time gigs that pay under the table, no matter what your brother tells you. You might very well get a job, but it's almost certainly going to be of the hand, blow, foot, or rim variety.

Eventually, I stumbled on something called "Executive Protection." It was interesting because it paid well. It was exciting because, while it supposedly leaned on some of the skills I spent years honing in the military, it was definitely *not* PMC work. In that sense it was comfortable and familiar, and it allowed me to keep telling myself that my struggle to acclimate was the climate's fault, not my own.

I put out feelers to all the private security firms in Southern California that I could find and eventually landed with one in downtown Los Angeles. I had to sign an NDA when I was on-boarded, so I can't tell you exactly who hired me, but what I can tell you is that being able to tell their clients that they were sending over someone who was former special operations was a huge bonus for this particular firm, which specialized in round-the-clock protection for wealthy families and high-dollar executives who regularly did business in countries that don't like to play by the rules.

Initially, I picked up one-off gigs here and there. I'd do security at red carpets or accompany an actress to an event after her stalker got released from the hospital. Nothing too weird, at least by L.A. standards. Eventually, I was assigned to an extremely wealthy family in Beverly Hills as part of a four-man detail that would rotate in twelve- to eighteen-hour shifts depending on what the family was doing any given week.

It took me a couple of months doing my best impression of a floor lamp to realize why the job paid as well as it did. It wasn't because of the risks I had to assume, it was because of all the shit I had to eat. And let me tell you, there was a *lot* of it. Every day it was Two Girls One Cup, and I was the cup. It's not that I hated this family—I didn't, they were nice people—but I was as much a piece of scenery as I was a part of their lives. If I hadn't carried a 9mm pistol and been carved from a solid block of American handsome, I suspect there would have been times they would have just tried to pick me up and move me themselves to eliminate any inconvenience my presence created.

It sounds more dehumanizing than it was, to be fair. The security firm prepares you for that aspect of the job. Nobody wants to feel like they're sharing their private living quarters with four perfect strangers. The entire goal of the job is to melt into the atmosphere and make your presence known only when the shit is going down. This wasn't *Man on Fire*. I wasn't Denzel trying to protect a little girl from a bunch of *narcotraficantes*. Though that would have been rad. Stateside kill!

What made the job difficult was that I never had an opportunity to show anyone what I could do. I was a creative guy, I was relatively smart, I liked to play music. But in this job that guy felt so far away—like a stranger. It didn't help that I hadn't cultivated any of these traits since high school, and no one I dealt with on the job was interested in digging in and pulling them out of me. *So, Mat, what do you like to do in your spare time? Do you have any hobbies or interests?* I don't know what I would have done if they *had* taken an interest, because in my mind, if I was being honest with myself, I was still a warfighter. Full stop. But was that *all* I was? Was that going to be what defined me for the rest of my life, *this fucking war?* Judging by my interactions with L.A. girls and Northridge college kids and my security firm, it seemed like that was a real possibility.

I pride myself on my work ethic. No matter what the job is, I want to go the extra mile and do the best damn job possible. In my old line of work, that meant being proficient in every weapons system, having my entire team prepared for every mission, and being in peak physical shape. In this job, it meant wiping down the windshield of the family's Bentley so they couldn't tell it had just passed by the sprinklers on the way up the driveway. It meant that when my boss, who was a major studio executive, invited all his famous friends over for Monday Movie Night, I helped move couches into the theater room without nicking any of the walls.

You have no idea how disorienting all this was. I was a twenty-four-year-old veteran with five combat tours in active war zones. I had led teams of *actual* heroes into firefights multiple times a week for months on end. *I had done shit.* The Army spent months, if not years, turning guys like me into perpetual motion machines of confidence, capability, and resolve. Yet after barely a year in Los Angeles, the Rambo sensibility and confidence that carried me through years of combat had all but disappeared, leaving me in a rage-filled, booze-soaked hole of self-doubt.

When you spend years within a tight-knit community fighting side by side, and you come from a long line of veterans who've served, it's not uncommon to hear stories about guys you know who struggle with doubt and depression. I knew that what I was dealing with—even if I couldn't put my finger on it at the time—was nothing new. Even the way it came about was nothing out of the ordinary. It was the accumulation of small, unexpected, unfamiliar, uncomfortable events that slowly began to take their toll. And what made it even weirder, and worse, was that all this was happening in fucking Los Angeles. I had gone directly from having one of the realest, most authentically important jobs imaginable to living in one of the fakest, vainest places on the planet.

Looking back, it's incredibly mind-blowing how quickly that town can break you down. The selfishness, rudeness, and disrespect that oozed from so many people in L.A. just going about their day doing absolutely nothing with their lives made me alternately furious and depressed. I knew that the shittiness I personally endured wasn't deliberate or overtly directed, but so many of these douchebags in their Sweet Sixteen convertibles and Mercedes G-wagons would just as soon run me over by accident as look right through me on purpose. Forget about Fort Rucker, the Army should move SERE (Survival, Evasion, Resistance, Escape) School here. Set the headquarters at Urth Caffé on Melrose, where they've mastered the art of pretending you don't even exist, and let only the strongest survive. Let the rest wonder, as I did, what the hell was I doing here?

Chapter 13

Party Patrol

My last day in private security was actually at night. I had a day off from my regular gig, and I was recommended for another job doing security for after-hours parties at a house in the Hollywood Hills. As was customary, the owner of the house wanted to meet and interview me. The email I received with all the details said to come up to the house where I'd be working around 11 P.M. I called the owner's assistant to see if the listed time was a typo. That couldn't be right.

"Hi, this is Mat Best. I'm calling to confirm a meeting this Thursday. It says to be there at 11 P.M. That's supposed to be 11 A.M., right?"

"No. 11 P.M. is right. Actually, I'm surprised it's that early," the assistant said.

She sounded high as shit.

"Excuse me?"

"Yeah, Goush usually wakes up at 10 P.M., so this is unusual. It's typically way later. He must be really mad about the flamingo incident."

10 P.M.? Goush? Flamingos?

In the Rangers, it was understood that some combatants could provide valuable intelligence that might help us do our job better moving forward, so it didn't always make sense to kill everything we saw. In this case, the guy's assistant had tipped her hand that she was in possession of valuable information that would make doing this job much easier, so I didn't hang up on her.

"Tell me about the flamingo incident," I asked, trying not to sound either excited by the ridiculousness or amused by the excesses of men like Goush.

"Ughhhhhh, so much fucking drama. Goush bought this statue of a rare South African flamingo at an auction, and someone broke the head off of it and threw it in the pool. He's been like, literally, destroyed over it. He wants security ASAP."

"Got it. I'll be there at 11 P.M., then."

"Right on," she said.

"Please extend my sincerest condolences to the flamingo too."

"Thank you. He'll appreciate that."

What the fuck is wrong with the people in this city? Who buys a flamingo statue in Africa and carts it halfway around the world to put next to a pool? This thing must be made out of rhino horn and panda whiskers.

The next night, I drove as far up into the Hollywood Hills as one can go without falling over the other side. I pulled up in front of a long driveway right at 11 P.M. A valet met me at the driver's-side door, ready to take my keys.

"Hey man, I'm here for a meeting. I can just park in the driveway."

"I wouldn't recommend it," he said.

"Why not?"

"If you're parked in the driveway after the party starts, you'll never get out of here. You'll be blocked in ten cars deep."

"There's a party tonight?"

All the valet guys started laughing. "There's a party here *every* night."

"What does Goush do?" I asked.

"No one knows," he said. "Here's your ticket."

I handed him my keys, took my ticket, and stepped out of my truck, slightly confused. As I headed up the driveway, the house looked like something out of *Scarface*. It was the biggest house I'd ever seen. The hill it was set into was so steep that you really couldn't appreciate the size and scope of it from the bottom of the driveway.

Goush was a fucking baller.

When I got to the front door and rang the doorbell, I was greeted by a hot blonde girl in her early twenties wearing a nearly see-through lingerie thing with no bra. This being L.A., she was either a girlfriend or the assistant—those were the only two reasonable possibilities—so I immediately diverted my eyes and gave a polite wave to hedge my bets.

"Hey, if this is a bad time, I can come back if you guys are—"

"Are you Mat?"

"Yeah, I'm Mat." I extended my hand to shake hers.

"It's nice to meet you," she said, going in for a huge hug. "I'm Serena. We talked on the phone yesterday."

Assistant. Thank god. Eyes up and forward.

"Thank you for your service," she said. "My grandfather was in the Coast Guard, so I know how much you sacrifice. Were you in the Coast Guard, by any chance?"

"No, I was a Ranger, but it's very similar," I said, just trying to get through this conversation and into the interview portion of the competition.

"A Ranger, huh? Fucking Texas is a crazy state. I bet you've seen some shit."

"Yup. Is Goush here?"

"Yeah, sorry. Look at me all fawning out over a Texas war hero. Sorry. We don't see too many military dudes in this town."

"You don't say?"

"No. Camo is hot this season, but these boys don't look like you. Goush is down in the pool house. Just walk all the way through and out the back."

"Thanks."

Serena re-hugged me as I left, and then bowed with her hands together, like every L.A. person does to veterans they meet for the first time. They think we're a mystical breed of human or something. When they see one up close, all motor skills completely shut down and they turn into yoga instructors. *Namaste.*

Walking through Goush's house, past endless paintings by artists I didn't know (and he probably didn't either), I heard the faint sounds of techno wafting from the back of his never-ending compound. If the apocalypse ever happens, find out where Goush lives and head there. You'll be all set.

When I finally made it out back, I was greeted by an infinity pool and the most amazing view of Los Angeles I'd ever seen. The city lights were so spectacular, it almost seemed fake. It reminded me of those big wide shots of L.A. that you see in TV shows and movies like *Heat* or *Collateral* or *Blade Runner.* I wouldn't be surprised if Goush rented this place out to studios just so they could get those shots. It was beautiful and at the same time bittersweet.

I was nearly two years into this private security job and nothing had really changed with the family I worked for full-time. It wasn't worse, it wasn't better, and it wasn't like there was room for advancement up the corporate ladder. What was I going to become, executive furniture mover? Head car-door opener?

At the same time, the relationship I'd been in was coming to an end. Let's just say her name rhymed with "Awful Person," since that's what she was. Awful Person was from Southern California (like so many other awful people I was set to encounter). We met on my final block leave, just before I got out of the Army and just after she'd gotten out of a long-term relationship. She was a good-looking girl, and we hit it off right away. She was like, "Fuck kids, fuck marriage," and I was like, "Great, so let's just fuck, then?" We started dating almost immediately, and she moved in with me in North Hollywood about six months later, because I am a stupid man and she had decided to stuff all her awfulness in a box that she buried deep in her closet full of skeletons. Fresh out of the military, unsure of what's next, you can't hook into a relationship and accelerate it like that. You're putting too much pressure on it. You're expecting it to paper over all the cracks that start to show up in your life when you don't have the same kind of purpose to get up for anymore.

It also didn't help the relationship that she fucked her ex-boyfriend a bunch of times while we were together. Side note: I believe they got married and he joined the military. Congrats! (Oh, and thanks for reading my book. I hope it moves you as much as your mouth moves when you read it #RLTW.)

What I needed was to break the lease on our shitty North Hollywood apartment and move into my own place. Unfortunately, I was working so much that I didn't have time to house hunt, which meant I was stuck—in the apartment, in the relationship, in the job.

Anyway, I was lost in these miserable thoughts, staring out at the beautiful view, when the DJ dropped the beat and a blast of shitty techno yanked me back to reality. Like with overpressure from automatic weapons fire, it took me a second to orient to the source of the music that was now overwhelming my senses. It was coming from the guesthouse off to the right of the pool. I cautiously knocked on a slightly cracked door to announce my presence. If the half-naked assistant is what I got at the front door, I had no idea what to expect once I got to the back.

"Hello? Mr. Goush?"

"Come on in!" someone screamed out over the music.

I opened the door and walked in to find a sweaty white man DJing behind a set of turntables. He nodded his head without stopping the music.

"Are you Mr. Goush?"

"What?" he said as he pulled off his headphones.

"I said, Are you Mr. Goush?"

"Fuck, no. I'm his personal DJ."

"I'm sorry, I wasn't aware that was an actual thing."

"Goush is in the bathroom. He'll be right out."

"WHY DID THE FUCKING MUSIC STOP?" someone yelled out from the bathroom.

Moments later a small Middle Eastern man emerged from the bathroom wearing a robe, slippers, and one tiny gold chain. He was wide-eyed with fury, though I'm pretty sure a pharmacy worth of drugs was most responsible for the giant saucers in his eye sockets.

This was Goush.

"Are you the American hero?" he said, with that indecipherable Middle Eastern accent that has become super common in Los Angeles. Is it Iranian? Is it Persian? Armenian? Lebanese? Who knows! All that mattered in this instance is that it was attached to the hairy little man who wanted to pay me to patrol his parties.

"I'm not a hero, just was in the military, sir."

"Don't you fuck me, man! I see you GI Joes on the plane when I go back overseas. You are a hero for dealing with those animals."

"Um, thanks?"

"No, thank you! Thank you for coming, man! Shit, you look too pretty to be security. Look at this," he said to the DJ. "They send Goush an Abercrombie model to work security, do you believe that?"

"That's crazy, Goush," he said in a monotone voice.

"Don't ever stop playing the fucking music again, you understand? Otherwise, I'll pay someone else to push play on their laptop for five grand a week. Hero, come with me."

Goush was clearly a complete lunatic, but at least he was funny. He led me out to the infinity pool and pointed down to the water. We stood there in silence for a moment. I could tell he was troubled.

"You see that?"

"What?" I responded.

"Down there, in the water. The head."

I squinted and leaned down closer to the water. Upon closer examination, I could see the head and long neck of a flamingo statue. Why were we here? Did he want me to dive in there and get it? Did he want me to eulogize the fucking thing? I didn't know what to do.

"I'm sorry for your loss," I said, finally. "May he or she rest in peace."

"Kimberley. That's what I named her. In South Africa, that's the name of the town where they breed. Beautiful flamingos, best I've seen on the planet. Have you been there?"

"No. I haven't gotten the chance."

"I have. I love flamingos. I paid a fortune for this piece, only to have it destroyed by two guys in a fight. Those fuckers, man. Have you seen gay guys fight?"

"Unfortunately, sir, that one is still on my bucket list." We laughed. Then he got serious.

"Do you think you could stop gay guys in a fight?"

"Uh, sure. That wouldn't be a problem. They're just dudes."

"They're fucking crazy. Watch out. That's why I need someone tough. A real man. Not a bullshit man."

"Are you saying you want to hire me to stop gay men from fighting?"

"Yes! That's exactly what I want, hero. They run around town and suck each other's dicks, then they get jealous about it and fight everywhere. They are like this with everything: fighting, fucking, dressing, talking the shit. They have no rules!" Apparently Mr. Goush was an amateur sociologist. "But they bring the hottest girls, so what are you going to do?" And a philosopher too.

When I encountered that National Guard unit outside the wire a couple years earlier, the experience helped me realize that being immersed in Ranger culture for four straight years had affected how I saw the world and, more to the point, how the world saw me. It was an enlightening and humbling experience. In fifteen minutes with Goush, my worldview was upended again. I wasn't sure if I was even calibrated properly to the *earth*, let alone civil society. *What in the motherfuck is going on here?* Goush could sense my indecision.

"I tell you what," he said. "Tonight you don't work. Tonight you party with Goush, okay?"

"I don't know," I said reflexively. I couldn't cite it from memory, but I was pretty sure there was a page somewhere in the conduct section of my firm's employee handbook that listed "Getting fucked up with the client" in the *Don't* column.

Then, out of my peripheral vision, I spotted Goush's assistant, Serena, walking out of the main house with three other unbelievably hot girls, all dressed like her, which is to say . . . barely. I pride myself on being professional, on staying mission-focused and on getting the job done, but there are times when certain circumstances come together in your life that you just have to say "Send it." Besides, technically, I didn't have the job yet, so Goush wasn't a client and I wasn't on the clock.

"Yeah, I think I'll stay and hang out for a bit."

"I fucking knew it, hero! You want any coke?"

"No thanks, I don't touch the stuff."

"I like it! Got to stay sharp mentally. If you need any, well, it's fucking everywhere. Just ask somebody." And with that, Goush started to walk back toward the main house. I stopped him before he got swallowed up by the techno.

"Hey, can I ask what you do for a living?"

"Little bit of jewelry, little bit of gold, little bit of oil." *Who is this guy, the fourth wise man?* "Family businesses. My fucking family is crazy!" He laughed as he passed the four girls on his way into the house and smacked one of them on the ass. She giggled and wagged her head, like sexual harassment was totally part of the employment contract.

"I fucking love America!" Goush screamed.

At least we have that in common, I thought.

Within minutes, the four scantily clad chicks grabbed me and pulled me into the pool house where the DJ was playing.

And for the next hour, I sat on a couch, drank top-shelf whiskey and watched the girls dance with each other in a twisting blizzard of sheer lingerie that made me feel like I was sitting inside a mosquito net hung from the ceiling by eight large fake tits. One by one they would each disappear into the bathroom and crush rails, just like their boss. As the night progressed, more and more people started to file in, each girl hotter than the last. As a young, virile twenty-four-year-old, I thought this whole scene was pretty awesome, but the part of me that was used to being responsible for the lives of young people wanted to sit down with every one of them and ask, "So, tell me about your relationship with your father. Do you think this is going to end well for you?"

Around 3 A.M., things started getting really hazy. I was eight or ten glasses deep into a bottle of Macallan 25 Year (still one of my personal faves) and the four humpsketeers were really flying. Two of them started making out. Serena watched me staring at them.

"You like that?"

"I mean, I definitely don't *dislike* it."

"I've never fucked a guy in the military before . . . and neither have they," she said as she pointed to the girls making out.

"Well," I said, "when it comes to protecting my country, I am obligated to go above and beyond the call of duty." Also on top, underneath, and behind it. Having been recently cheated on, my moral compass was pointing due south, straight into my pants.

"You guys want to have sex with a real Texas Ranger?" she shouted to her friends.

"That's not what I—" But before I could finish my sentence, they grabbed my arms, pulled me off the couch, and led me to a guest room in the pool house.

I could hear the DJ's music pounding through the adjacent wall. For the next I don't know how many hours, through the night and into the morning, I was in and out of consciousness as often as I was in and out of these girls. It never ended, because I had the meanest case of whiskey dick of all time. I was like a half-inflated hot air balloon: I had enough in me to stay aloft, but not so much that you could fire the burner and bring the whole thing in for a safe landing. We were all going to crash and burn eventually, it was just a matter of when.

As the sun started to peek through the windows the next morning, I heard voices screaming outside. I looked at the wall and noticed a flamingo clock—nice touch, Goush—that read 7:00 A.M. *Holy shit!* Then I heard a loud smack followed by an even louder scream. I got up out of bed, threw on my silkies, and went out to see what was going on.

Walking through the pool house, I found the DJ sleeping on the floor underneath his turntables while the music kept pumping from his MacBook. This dude was literally a slave to the beat. I rubbed my eyes and walked toward the door. Another vicious slap echoed off the hillside.

"Fuck you, Jeremy!"

I picked up the pace and ran outside. I couldn't believe my eyes. It was two gay guys fighting! They saw me see them, then started screaming and slapping the shit out of each other full bore. I ran over to break it up, pushing them away from each other like a middle school vice principal, and just like a couple of middle school jackasses, one of them thought it would be wise to disobey me. The guy I assumed was Jeremy tried to charge right through me. *No sir. That is not going to happen. I don't care how great your pecs are.* I grabbed him and put him in a rear naked choke.

If you've never seen someone get choked out at a party, it can be kind of a boner killer. Unless, of course, it's your party.

"I fucking knew you were the guy!" a voice screamed down from the main house. "Fuck yes, hero! You're hired!"

I looked up to find Goush hanging halfway out his bedroom window, completely naked. I released Jeremy from the chokehold and slowly lowered his limp body to the pool deck. The guy he was fighting ran over hysterically crying as Jeremy came to. He held Jeremy's head in his lap, and then they kissed and embraced, like nothing had happened. *Wait, these guys are together? That was a coked-out lover's quarrel? Over what?*

What the fuck is happening with my life?

I walked back into the pool house and grabbed my clothes.

"Hey, why are you leaving?" Serena said in a groggy voice. "You should stay. I have some Xanax, we could sleep in." How's that for pillow talk?

"I can't, but thanks. I've got to get back to Texas with the rest of my Rangers. You understand."

"Oh, totally. You were amazing, my Texas Ranger."

I did a fake tip of my invisible cowboy hat and got dressed. On the way down the driveway, the same valet was leaning next to his stand, smiling at me. He handed me my keys and laughed.

"See you tomorrow," he said.

"I don't think so."

"Everyone comes back."

"Not me."

Driving back to my apartment, I could feel myself nearing rock bottom. This city had lost its soul, and it was starting to take mine with it. I'd just spent twelve hours with a bunch of people who were *existing*, bouncing from one stimulus to the next, with no intention and nothing to show for it. On top of that, I was now headed home to a girlfriend I actively disliked and had not been getting along with for at least a year. This was not me. I am a work-horse. I act with purpose. I don't do . . . whatever the fuck it is I just did up there in the hills. At least not for a paycheck or to prove myself to anyone. I did not recognize this version of myself.

And that was the most frightening aspect of it all. When you've lost track of the person you were proud to be for all those years, who cares what happens to whatever is left in his place? He could go crazy, he could go nowhere, he could go to hell. What's the difference? I spent five tours dedicated to killing bad guys, and now the baddest guy of all was the voice in the head of the person looking back at me in the rearview mirror. When I pulled into my parking spot at the apartment complex, I couldn't move. I sat there in my car for an hour and a half, trying to figure out what to do. Finally, I pulled out my phone and called my dad.

"Dad, is that studio you rent out available? I've got to get the fuck out of this place."

He could sense the urgency in my voice. "It's rented, but I'll get them out by the end of the month. Until then, I'll have a bed ready for you. Come on home."

That's all I needed to hear. I jumped out of my truck, walked into my apartment, broke up with Awful Person, packed up all my shit, and hit the 101 Freeway up to Santa Barbara.

It was an important step, but I knew it was only the first one of many. I didn't just need to get out of Los Angeles, I needed to get out of California, out of this funk. It was time to find some purpose in my life. To find something that would remind me of who I was again.

Chapter 14

When Life Gives You an Ox, Make Oxen

Back in Santa Barbara, my days were smooth and easy, if a little monotonous. My nights, however, were the exact opposite. I was still going out with friends and getting obliterated, but for the first time since leaving the Army, I was getting into bar fights again. I never started any of them—even back at Fort Lewis—and I always tried to defuse situations with my words. I would go so far as to buy shots for the guy or guys causing the problem in an attempt to be the peacemaker. But I was equally clear with myself where my line was and that if it was crossed, people were getting punched.

In recent weeks, that line seemed to be moving closer and closer in. There were fewer whiskey shots and more kidney shots. I was putting as many good dudes into taxis as I was putting dickheads into hospitals. To be fair, beach towns like Santa Barbara and San Diego breed a particular kind of drunk douchebro who knows exactly which buttons to push to get his fucking ass beat.

One night, this young kid was just absolutely Kiefer Sutherland drunk, and he was talking an endless stream of shit to me and my friends. I can handle shit-talking, even the kind that doesn't stop. You just smile, nod, and ignore. Basically you treat them like they're your parents. The problem was, this kid hated to be ignored, so when he realized that his antics weren't getting a rise out of any of us, he started putting hands on people, which was well across my personal line. I have no clear memory of how we got outside, since I had found my way to the bottom of a Jameson bottle by that point, but what I do remember was this kid rushing me with his head down, me putting him into a Muay Thai clinch and kneeing his face into oblivion, then his head bouncing off the sidewalk like one of those Bozo the Clown inflatable punching bags. How that kid was not dead and I am not in jail right now is a legitimate miracle. I would thank God for my luck if I wasn't at least 50 percent sure that the real reason this kid didn't sustain a life-changing TBI was that he didn't actually have a *B* to *I*.

At the same time, I started dreaming of being back overseas, at war. Once I'd get home from the bar and pass out, my subconscious mind devoted night after night to churning through my past experiences, reliving them—not as nightmares but as *fantasies*. The dreams were as exhilarating as they were disturbing, quickly escalating in frequency and intensity.

Then one day I got a call from my old Ranger buddy Trey Bullock. Trey was one of the guys who had gotten out of the Army right around the time I did and went straight into private contracting work. He'd just returned stateside from being deployed and was calling to check in. I told him everything that was going on with me and he suggested that I reach out to the subcontracting outfit that was employing him. He said that if I wanted, he could help streamline the processing of a new security clearance so I could enroll in their qualification course in time for their next contract.

It was the best news I'd heard in nearly two years. This was the solution to everything I'd been missing and everything I was struggling to deal with. I'd avoided this immediately after getting out of the Army, but now I was ready. I'd have a place to put all this furious emotional energy. I'd be back with a team. And I'd be back doing something I was really good at, back being a part of something with *meaning*.

The million-dollar question was: Did I still have it?

The list of requirements you have to meet before you can even apply for a contracting position with the ███ is, to paraphrase the

great Nick "Goose" Bradshaw, "long and distinguished." You need
to be a combat veteran; you need to have served in a Special Operations unit; you need to be able to obtain a specific level of clearance . . . the list goes on. As a result, the selection criteria, if you've
been allowed to apply, are oriented primarily toward the attributes
of guys who had been "operators" for some period of time: physical fitness, marksmanship, close quarters combat, that kind of
thing. Although drunken nights that ended at In-N-Out Burger
were a regular part of my stint as a private security manny, I made
sure I was in *animal-style* shape by the time I applied to the program and was allowed to go through my qualification course on
the East Coast.

Selection starts with a PT test that consists of a mile-long run,
followed by a 100-meter 200-pound dummy drag, and finishes
with another three-quarter-mile run. All of this you have to complete in less than thirteen minutes. I could sit here and articulate
why you should think I'm an awesome badass because I met some
sort of physical standard to be a ███████████████, but in reality,
like everything in life, success starts with not being a pussy. Put
one foot in front of the other, recognize that no matter what, all
adversity will end at some point, and then smile to the poor son-
of-a-bitch who is struggling worse than you when you pass him on
the way to the finish line.

Most people qualified for this kind of contracting work don't
have issues with the PT test, but if there is one part that smokes
people more than the others, it's dragging that fucking dummy. I
think the reason it catches people by surprise is that Jonathan Sil-
verman and Andrew McCarthy made it look so easy in *Weekend at
Bernie's*. Make no mistake, though: It's a bitch. If you forget to
hydrate or stretch, you can very easily cramp up and collapse to
the ground. When the dehydration is really bad, it looks a lot like
an epileptic seizure. It's scary if you've never seen it happen before. If you have, then it's just hilarious.

After the PT test, they put us through the standard push-up/sit-
up/pull-up challenge. Most everyone in my selection group had
been in Special Operations, so this was old hat. You want me to

burn out my arms and back and core for no particular reason? Fine. As long as I don't have to sit down in a frozen swamp afterward, I'll Lionel Richie this motherfucker and go all night long.

Once you've met these basic physical standards, that's when the course officially starts. It's a few weeks of training during which you go through a wide variety of scenarios in order to learn the organization's tactics, techniques, and procedures. This consists of firearms training and qualification, close quarters combat training, driving school, fight training, and a long list of other fun stuff that involves being a man. If you show up on time, meet the standards, and don't quit, at the end you get a nice little certificate. It's like a Bachelor's of Badassery.

One of my favorite pieces of training that we conducted during qualification was called the hooded box drill. Surprisingly, the name says it all. The drill begins in an empty room in which you are placed inside a four-foot-by-four-foot square box that has been taped off on the ground. You are given an M4 and a Glock 19 loaded with simunition and told that you cannot exit the box at any time during the drill. Next they turn on really loud music and bring a hood down over your head so you can't see anything. While you listen to something that sounds like Edward Scissorhands fingerbanging a Vitamix turned up to 11, the instructors cook up whatever interesting scenario they can think of. When the instructors are ready, the mask comes flying off your head and you are presented with a situation that you have to react to instantaneously. Maybe someone in a safety suit immediately punches you in the face as four other combatants go for your limbs. Maybe they all open up on you with AK-47 simunitions. The details don't matter; the important thing is that the drill induces high levels of stress in order to test your ability to react appropriately in a highly volatile situation.

The key to the whole exercise is the simunitions. These fun little guys resemble standard 5.56 and 9mm rounds, but the bullet tips are plastic and filled with paint. They are designed to bring a more realistic approach to training by delivering a healthy dose of pain. As someone who has been shot with simunitions more than his fair share of times, let me assure you that they fucking hurt. (The ass cheek and the belly button are the worst places to get hit.) Taking a few shots wasn't a bad trade-off, though, because it meant not only would I be able to barrel check someone's face and shoot others with my own simunitions, but also, if I did it well enough, I might actually get a job out of it. What is that thing people say: If you do what you love, you'll never work a day in your life? I didn't fully understand that old chestnut until I got to put the quad rail of an M4 into the nose of some asshole dressed like a Rock 'Em Sock 'Em Robot.

The drill is as chaotic and terrifying as it sounds—more so, probably. Still, some guys cleared their scenarios with relatively few bumps or bruises and sailed through this portion of the course. The ones who freaked out got pretty banged up. And if they couldn't get back in there and pass the standard, well, they got dropped.

Although the training is taken very seriously, we always found a way to fit in some fun. In this line of work, you have to. So after completing simunitions training, we walked over to a joint facility that had just installed a brand-new Live Wall. A Live Wall is a simulated firing range that outfits you with a fake gun connected to a CO_2 backpack that produces the kickback of a normal firearm and registers the hits of your "bullets" through infrared technology. Essentially, it's a four-dimensional video game—time is a factor—with real-world mechanics. For kicks, the instructors had us do what they call in the biz an "El Presidente," which is a speed drill to test firing accuracy. You start out with your back to a target, and the instant you hear a *ding* you turn and fire five shots in the center of a human silhouette as quickly as you can.

Before I go any further, let me just reiterate, once again, that this was *for fun*. Let me also clarify that, yes, I understand that the standard drill calls for two shots to the chest and one to the head. If all you keyboard warriors out there don't mind, why don't you do me a favor and holster your mice for a few minutes and get back to 4chan while I finish with my sweet training story.

When everyone had their turn at El Presidente, the instructors had us run through one of the most basic programs on the Live Wall: two silhouette targets, ten meters away. The goal was to see who could shoot the best and the fastest. By definition, the person who won would be the shooter with the best firing mechanics and the best target acquisition. Now, I wasn't going into it trying to demoralize people, but as a former Ranger who takes pride in being a rifleman first (and in being the most competitive person on the planet), once this thing turned into a competition, I was in it to win it.

It wasn't pretty. I ran through the entire class and smoked everyone with my dominant hand . . . *twice*.

"What the fuck, man?" said one of the instructors. It's not like I did any Wild Bill shit, but they clearly weren't used to seeing the kind of proficiency I could bring to bear with a gun in my hand. I think they were worried that their pretty little Live Wall might be malfunctioning.

"If you want, I can switch guns and run through it left-handed instead?" I offered.

"Be fucking serious."

"I'm down, sir."

"I'd *love* to see that happen," he said, playing along.

The instructor must have thought I was joking or something. I wasn't. I can shoot with equal proficiency right-handed and left-handed. Along with impeccable beard maintenance, it's one of those life skills that I take very seriously. The gun was the primary tool of the trade for the majority of my adult life to that point. It was the difference between life and death—for me, sure, but more importantly for my team—and to not be as good as I could possibly be with it felt like it would have been a betrayal.

I ran through the course again, this time using my left hand, and beat every single person again.

"What kind of hotdog shit was that?" the instructor demanded to know as I headed back to the group.

"The kind you *relish*?" I asked. If you need me, I'll be serving three to five in the punitentiary.

"You think that's funny? Would you do that in combat?"

"Actually, I have."

"Oh, would you look at the golden boy over here. Thank you for gracing us with your presence today," he said as he mockingly slow-clapped for me. "The fucking poster child."

People stared at me like I was an asshole. Some of them wanted to beat my ass, probably because they felt like they had gotten hustled. Who knew normal, humble Mat was such a cocky, ruthless, dead-eyed competitor? Others were just deflated, because they didn't think this kind of thing was possible. You can't be ruggedly handsome *and* a sharpshooter.

The reality is that I have always taken my shooting extremely seriously. I trained for years to be able to shoot with both hands and, eventually, to win a Ranger Battalion company stress shoot. The reason I was able to pull off this little stunt wasn't because of any innate superpower. I just had the patience and motivation that most people don't have, quite frankly, to put in the metric shit ton of work it takes to be great at something. To this day, I'm at the range three to four times a week when I'm home, keeping my shit tight. That's not to say I've never been bested at shooting. Of course I have, don't be ridiculous. It's a humbling experience. But if you learn from your shortcomings and train even harder for the next go-round, it will only lead to higher performance.

The Live Wall represented the end of the shooting portion of qualification school. When we wrapped, they split us up into groups of six, loaded us into white commercial passenger vans, and sent us up the road to some run-down small town for the final portion of the selection process, fight school. I can't imagine being a full-time resident of that town. Every two weeks a bunch of jacked, bearded dudes cycle through, invade the local bars and restaurants, and tell anyone who asks, "Yeah, I'm an accountant" or "I'm a bible salesman."

The fun part about contracting is that you meet people from all over the spectrum of professional badassery. Army Rangers, Marine Raiders, Army Special Forces (a.k.a. Green Berets), Navy

SEALs, and whatever other testosterone-filled face-shooting profession you can think of that isn't cumshot porn. Most of the dudes
in my van were former Special Operations, and except for me all
of them had a gig confirmed already. They were just going through
the motions in order to requalify and deploy. This created a bond
and a quick, easy comfort level among the group, the kind where
you already have each other's backs. Where you can finish each
other's sentences and answer each other's questions before they've
been asked.

"How long is this—"

"Four fucking hours to the hotel," one of the guys answered as
the driver closed the sliding passenger door behind us.

"You know what would be—"

"Beers."

"For the road."

"Yes."

"Totally."

"Put it inside me—"

"Right fucking now."

We had four hours to kill, and we didn't have to report to fight
school until 7 A.M. the next day, so what was the harm in a few
beers with your new buddies? Well, when it's a bunch of Special
Operations guys in a van, there's *plenty* of possible harm.

We had the driver pull over at the next available convenience
store. We walked in and stared into the bottom-lit beverage cool-
ers. Row after row of cans and bottles stared back at us, all of
them in cardboard boxes covered in primary colors specifically
designed to appeal to guys like us who move their lips when they
read. One of the guys started bobbing his head like he was in the
middle of a telepathic call-and-response with all the advertising.

"You guys thinking what I'm—"

"A thirty-pack apiece?" I asked.

"Yuuuuup."

The driver—a fellow student who had been tasked with being
the designated driver—stayed in the car for what I assume was
plausible deniability. He started laughing and shaking his head

when we came marching out of the store a few minutes later, each of us carrying an ice-cold brick of freedom, like we just walked out of the poster for *Three Kings*. Being an American is about celebrating diversity, so naturally we had everything from Natty Ice to Budweiser under our arms. For the fancy import lovers in our group, we even picked up some champagne of beers, Miller High Life. We were officially in business. When we were finally all back in the van, the driver slammed his door shut, turned, and looked at us hard.

"One, don't offer me a beer. I gotta stay sober, because this is going to be a shit show. Two, I'm not stopping for piss breaks. You either hold it in or find another way. We good with those rules?"

"Easy day," I said. Everyone either agreed or didn't care.

The second we pulled out of the parking lot, all six of us cracked open cans of beer in unison. It was a symphony for alcoholics inside a van for crazy people. We spent the next hour or so laughing, talking about girls, and telling crazy fucked-up war stories. It was everything I loved about being in the Army and everything I missed while pretending to be furniture in Los Angeles. I finally felt like myself again . . . which is why I had no problem being the first one to pull his dick out and piss into one of the empty cans rolling around on the floor.

Once I broke the seal, every single other dude grabbed an empty can and followed suit. It was the quietest the van had been since we left the convenience store. The eerie silence caused the driver to look in his rearview mirror to see what was going on. What he saw was the fountains at Bellagio, in miniature and with urine. It was majestic and probably horrifying, which inspired him to jerk the wheel, fishtailing the van and making most of us piss on ourselves. Any piss we didn't catch landed on the van's rubber floor mats.

"Sorry about that, boys," he said with a smile. "Armadillo. Didn't want to hit it."

When we finally got to the hotel, everyone wanted to continue the party. Fight school was kind of a joke. They don't really do anything there that most of us haven't already done. The worst that could happen is that we sloppily go through the motions, puke on ourselves, and get our hangovers punched out of our heads in the process. So why not enjoy ourselves? I walked up to the young female receptionist at the front desk to check in and tried to maintain whatever level of sobriety I had left.

"Excuse me, ma'am, after we get our keys, these lovely gentlemen and I are looking for your finest local watering hole."

"There's a bar next door," she said, without even looking up from her keyboard, "but I would recommend showering first, because you guys smell like a urinal."

"I'm sorry, in what sense?" I asked.

"In every possible sense imaginable," she said in a monotone voice as she faked a smile and processed our room keys.

We took the keys, and we did *not* take her advice. There would be no showering. We had worked hard to smell this bad. Instead, we threw our bags in our rooms and headed straight for the bar, where our presence was felt immediately. Most of the guys knew we were trouble and wanted nothing to do with us, so they quietly left. One of them didn't move an inch, however. His name was "Oxen." He was a student in our selection class who had taken another van up to the hotel. Apparently, we were not the only genius operators in this outfit, because Oxen's group had turned their van into a party bus as well. Oxen was already Irish-Catholic drunk, which says something because Oxen is, well, ox-sized. He was at least six-foot-four and had to clock in close to three hundred pounds, most of it that hard, lumpy man muscle you get from lifting heavy things and throwing them around a lot. He was as close to a real-life Paul Bunyan as you are going to get without an overactive pituitary gland. He was also the single most perfect representation of a Marine that I had ever met. Not the Marines from the television commercial, wearing dress blues in the middle of the desert catching lightning with their swords; I'm talking about actual jarhead, fuck-your-world-up Marines. Some might describe Oxen as the biggest knuckle-dragging dumbshit Marine you could possibly imagine, but I would quibble with that depiction. His arms weren't *nearly* that long.

Fortunately for us, girls that hang out at bars like this one aren't usually looking to hook up with guys who are built like a cement mixer. They much prefer guys like my crew—strong, agile operators who can fill a room with laughter and a cargo van with urine. When we walked in, all the single ladies looked at us like a batch of fresh meat in a town filled with zombie dicks, and they were *starving*.

Two girls who seemed as morally casual as they were fancily dressed (especially for a weekday) approached me and my Ranger buddy Lennon right away.

"Who are you guys?" one of them asked, all flirty.

"We're foreign aid workers," Lennon said. *Okay, I can work with that*.

"We're in town working on a well-drilling project to bring drinking water to starving African kids. It's all about the kids."

"Maybe you've heard of us," my buddy continued, "we're part of that clean water organization that Matt Damon founded."

"OhmigodIloveMattDamonhessoamazingohmigod," the other girl said without stopping to breathe. "*Courage Under Fire* is like my favorite E-VUH-ERR!"

The girls immediately hooked their arms in ours and led us out of the bar. It was like that scene in *Love Actually* when the goofy British ginger walks into some dive bar in Wisconsin and three hot chicks who love British accents surround him, take him to one of their houses, and basically rape him. Except in this case, instead of accents, it's military guys; and instead of taking us to their house, they led us across the parking lot to our hotel.

When we busted through the hotel door, they started screaming for us to take our shirts off. We obliged and they jumped on us, making out with us like the secret to happiness was at the bottom of our esophagus and the only way to get it was to fish it out with their tongues. We were well on our way to a winner-take-all pants-off dance-off when we heard a knock at the door.

"Hey, you guys!" said someone in a slow, half-joking manner.

It was Oxen.

I got up and opened the door.

"Oh shit, I'm sorry. I didn't know you guys were with girls," he said as he peeked into the room.

"No worries. What's up dude?"

"Nothing, I'm going down the street to get some beers at the store. You guys want anything?" Oxen asked.

"Naw, man. I'm all tapped out. I'm good," I said. "Lennon?"

"Yeah, man, tapped out here too."

"All right, cool. I'll get enough beers for everyone, anyway," he said as he bumped my fist and walked away down the hall.

"We'll hit you up later."

As the door shut, the girls began making out with us again, except now something felt sort of off about it, like they were just going through the motions, putting on a show. Suddenly, they jumped up.

"Hey guys, we're going to go to the vending machine to get some sodas, do you want anything?"

"No, I think we're good," I said. "We could go get soft drinks for you if you'd like? There's no need for you guys to go." I'm such a gentleman.

"No, it's okay," the girl said, looking over at her friend. "We don't know what we want yet, we'll be right back."

"Okay," I said, like a scorned lover in a Lifetime movie.

They got up quickly and left, pulling the door shut behind them. My buddy and I tried to assess the situation. Something was up, but . . . what? We were former Rangers and soon-to-be ███████████. Surely we had enough investigative chops between us to figure this shit out. On the other hand, we also had enough beer in us to drown triplets in a bathtub. So we waited. Five minutes went by. Then ten. I looked at my friend and turned off the television.

"Yo man, something is off here," I said, Sherlocking the shit out of our situation. All I needed was a cape and a cocaine addiction and I'd be ready to solve all sorts of crimes.

"You want to go look for them?" he said. "Their purses are here, so they definitely didn't leave."

"Yeah, let's do a little recon mission."

We threw on our shirts and bounced out of the room. The first stop was the vending machines. Nothing. Then we walked back across the parking lot to the bar. Nada. We wandered the halls of the hotel aimlessly, searching for our soulmates the way only two young drunk dudes on the precipice of pussy could. Empty-handed after like twenty minutes, we headed to the nearest elevator, ready to throw in the towel. That's when we heard loud female moans coming from the other end of the hall in what sounded like stereo. We immediately started walking toward the noise. As we got closer, and the moaning got louder, we could hear a male voice mixed in with the moans and the giggles. As we zeroed in on its source, I had a horrifying realization.

"Oh my God," I said to Lennon, "I think the noise is coming from Oxen's room." I took a step back to catch my breath.

"No way . . . you think?" he said, slowly coming to terms with what we were about to walk in on.

I knocked on the door.

"Just a sec!" Oxen said.

He answered the door out of breath, completely naked. Behind him, lying on top of a fully made hotel bed, also completely naked, were both of our girls, watching very loud porn while they masturbated. Between them on the bed was a large, Oxen-sized gap. I quickly gathered that the girls had not been the only ones masturbating when we knocked. My mind took those facts and spun them into a mental image that was the stuff of nightmares. Something your mind's eye can't *un-see*. If it weren't evening, I would have walked out into the middle of the parking lot and stared up into the sun until it baked my retinas and maybe, hopefully, if there is a God, erased this moment from my memory.

Oxen looked surprised but happy to see us. He flipped the deadbolt to keep the door from slamming shut and stepped into the hallway, still butt naked. "Hey guys, what's up?"

"Um, what's up is you're masturbating with the two girls we left the bar with," Lennon said.

"Oh, shit. I'm sorry, man. After I left your room, these girls came running after me and tracked me down as I was opening my door."

"I think maybe 'running' might be a bit of an exaggeration," I said, feeling very insecure in that moment.

"Well, they were moving pretty fast."

"Did they, like, want to fuck you?" Lennon asked. At this point, which one of us was more confused was a coin flip.

"I guess. It was super weird. They asked if they could come in and drink some beers. Then they wanted to watch some porn."

"And you didn't think that was strange?" I said.

"Not really. They said they wanted to hang for a bit, and they asked if they could have some cab money."

It was all starting to make sense. When we said we were tapped out, we meant for drinking, but they thought we meant money-wise. "How much?" I asked.

"Aw, just a couple hundred dollars apiece. They live like two hours away."

Cab money. Uh huh. Lennon and I smiled at each other.

"Prostitutes," Lennon said.

"What? Come on, guys. No way." Oxen seemed shocked. He looked back at them masturbating on the bed and hoped it wasn't true, but deep in his heart he knew. After a few seconds of self-reflection, he nodded at us and slowly shut the door.

"Whose credit card do you think that porn is being charged to?" Lennon said.

Great question. We let Oxen have this moment with his prosties, to make peace with his life choices and let karma settle the accounts. Then, after extensive teeth-brushing and deep-throating a bottle of Scope, we went to bed.

The next morning we were up and at 'em by 7 A.M. for fight school. One by one, we slogged out of our hotel rooms and made our way to the van beneath the unforgiving light of a sun that, only a few hours earlier, I was hoping might melt my brain like Icarus's wings. When we opened the van door, a beer bottle full of piss rolled out and smashed on the ground. Oh, that's right, we turned this van into an R. Kelly video yesterday.

"Guys, we have to clean this fucking van," I said. "If the instructors find out, we're going to get fired from a job we haven't even started." The group nodded in agreement.

"We have to be there in fifteen minutes," one of the guys said, "You got any suggestions?" In fact, as someone with extensive experience cleaning bodily fluids out of vehicles that don't belong to me, I did.

"We park far away. When we break for lunch, we Google the nearest car wash and pay them whatever the fuck they want."

When lunch hit, we drove to a nearby car wash and gave them extra for the best clean they could finish in the twenty minutes we had to spare. I've been less nervous for at-home pregnancy test results than I was sitting in their little reception area, waiting for the van to get pulled around. When the Mexican dude in charge handed the keys back to our driver, I opened the passenger door to inspect the results. The smell was still there. I looked over at *el jefe* like Sollozzo looked at Tom Hagan in *The Godfather* when he found out Vito Corleone had survived the assassination attempt. *"He's still alive. They hit him with five shots and he's still alive!"* I was beside myself. Then, out of the corner of my eye, I spotted a power washer leaning up against a wall.

"How much for that?" I said as I pointed at the power washer.

"You want *that*?"

"I need the big guns, man. You were in that van. Doesn't it smell like a bunch of drunk guys pissed everywhere because the driver kept on swerving back and forth when he saw that they were trying to piss into the empty beer cans that were laying all over the floorboards?"

"Yes, my friend, I wasn't going to say anything, but—"

"So how much for the power washer? I need it, man."

The floor was Rhino-lined and the mats were rubber. If anything was going to get this stench out, it was going to be a piping-hot load of pressurized water. Basically, an industrial-strength colonic.

"Forty dollars. But I can't do it for you, my friend. You have to do it yourselves. That thing could fuck up a vehicle if you're not careful."

"I appreciate the advice, but if we don't get the smell out of that vehicle, we're going to be the ones who get fucked up," I said as I handed him the forty dollars.

"Okay, okay. *Pinches gringos locos,*" he said under his breath. "Drive it around back and do it, so my boss doesn't see you."

After years of combat deployments, you learn how to assess and assume calculated risks. If I go here, this guy might go there. If I do this, that might happen. It's all part of the game, part of war, part of life. Unleashing a power washer inside a rented van was just another calculated risk, with a different set of assumptions and consequences.

Thankfully, it worked. The smell was gone and the van was spotless. We hopped back in, headed back to the fight school, and left the windows down so that the vehicle could air dry. The instructors never found out, and I was fortunate to finish and graduate. A few days later I got the call that I was cleared to deploy and the contracting gig was mine if I wanted it. For the first time in a couple years, I felt that I had purpose again, and I was thankful for that.

After a little more than two years away from active duty, there was something very satisfying about meeting and exceeding the selection criteria that the ████ used to vet its contractor candidates. It made me feel like I still had my mojo and wasn't completely washed up. It was time to get after it again.

Chapter 15

The Hundred-Foot War

Contracting for the ██████ wasn't nearly as glamorous as it sounds. There were no J███████████████. No surreptitious meetings over Turkish coffee at a Parisian sidewalk café with your counterpart from the other side, out in the open. You didn't slide important documents across the table in a file folder with the agency label printed on top and CLASSIFIED stamped across the bottom.

Okay, I was half kidding. There is *some* cool shit you never get to hear about, like this one time when ████████████████████

████████████ I'M ████████████████████

████████████████████████████████████

████████████████ NOT ████████████████

████████████████████████████████████

████████████ TELLING ████████████████

████████████████████████████████████

████████████████████ YOU ████████████

████████████████████████████████████

████████████████████████████████ ANY

████████████████

In many ways, contracting is like working for any other government bureaucracy. There was lots of red tape, lots of "hurry up and wait," and a fair amount of "you better keep your goddamn receipts." Unlike my private security gigs back stateside, here the money was good explicitly because of the risk you were taking when you weren't sitting around counting the holes in the asbestos-filled ceiling tiles above your bed.

The major benefit of the job was that when you were done working for the day, your time was yours. You didn't have to conduct a bunch of busy work to pretend like you weren't wasting taxpayer dollars. Someone a little older and more mature might take advantage of this freedom to exchange emails with friends and family or start assembling a diversified stock portfolio—you know, grown-up shit. For someone my age, the downtime offered ample opportunity to find trouble. On one deployment, I managed to pull the biggest contracting no-no of them all: DO NOT HAVE SEX WITH A ███████████!*

Whoopsies.

In my defense, it wasn't entirely my fault. When an absolute smoke show appears before you like a mirage in the desert—a tiny oasis of beauty amidst an ugly, scarred landscape—asking a man of my particular makeup not to give in to his thirst is asking him to fight hundreds of thousands of years of human evolution. *I'm only one man!*

We met on the flight over to Kuwait from Washington, D.C. I remember looking at her for the first time on the plane and thinking, *There is no way a woman this pretty is deploying overseas.* Especially not to my little turd-infested corner of the litter box. But somehow, we were headed to the same place. She was a ███████████ with a call sign, which is about as hot as it gets. Her call sign was ██████ but I'm going to call her "Libra" because in astrology Libra's ruling planet is Venus, which rhymes with *penis,* which is basically what was ruling me when we met.

Libra was as whip-smart as she was filthy hot. What made her (and Wendy Peffercorn before her) so unusual wasn't that she was legitimately great-looking—that in itself is rare enough—it was that she was great-looking *and* in the ████ *and* single. That combination was the true oddity. There are virtually no good-looking women deployed overseas to begin with. If you meet one, she is almost always engaged or married. So when you get sent to some small base in the middle of nowhere and you meet a hot, single girl there—out of all the other possible people who could have been deployed in her position—she seems like a unicorn. And when you discover that unicorns are, in fact, real and there is one in your immediate vicinity, there's really only one thing you can do: try to have sex with it.

---

* Since this got redacted, I want to be clear that this was a human I fucked.

There were *so many* problems with this plan.

First, obviously, were the "rules." Sleeping with ██████████ ██████ is how many private security contractors lose their jobs, whether the ██████ is a wealthy divorcee or ██████. It's Rule Number One because it is often what gets in the way of Rule Number Two: DO YOUR JOB. I pride myself in doing my job and doing it well—that includes abiding all *relevant* rules and regulations—so I was going to make sure that we were always extremely professional. No matter how sneaky or cool you think you are, mistakes and carelessness get people killed. As much as I love pussy, and there's not a human alive who loves it more than me, it's not worth putting others' lives in jeopardy for, even when there is no imminent threat of danger toward your site. Not then, not ever. I could never live with myself if getting ass were to blame for getting shelled.

And people would have been looking to me if something like that occurred since I was the site team leader. That was probably the biggest risk of all when it came to hooking up with Libra, because it meant heightened scrutiny, especially at my age. Site team leader is a role that usually goes to much older guys, so there were a bunch of dudes who got super salty when they heard the job went to some kid who was barely twenty-six years old. To make matters worse, my call sign inside ████████████ and our contracting group was "Poster." As in *poster child*. I'd been christened with that fucking albatross of a nickname after Wild Billing my way through the marksmanship phase of the ██████ qualification course. Some of the guys ██████████████ knew that's where the name had come from, but most didn't, so they filled their knowledge gap with the least charitable assumptions possible. Maybe I was a general's son. Or maybe I was just some sniveling apple polisher who knew how to play politics. The possibility that I hustled my ass off, took every assignment that came my way without question, and was also good at my job I'm sure never crossed their minds. I certainly wasn't going to give them the satisfaction of telling them the truth. And even if I had, it wouldn't have done anything to remove the target on my back.

The logistics of hooking up were their own ball of bullshit. The size of the ██████████ rendered privacy more or less nonexistent. These ██████████████████████████████ are incredibly tiny. They usually hold fifty people at most and have the size and mentality of a rural middle school. Everyone knew everyone else's business. You could literally walk into the bathroom after a couple weeks and know, from the smell alone, exactly who had taken that shit and how long ago they had taken it. The irony was never lost on me that nobody on the outside really knew where I was going, but everyone on the inside knew what I was doing. And *who*.

Then there was the issue of where we could hook up. At least at █████ I could steal a truck and hide behind restaurants run by local contract employees who could give two shits about what I was up to. Here, it was Libra's ten-foot-by-ten-foot plywood-walled pod or nothing (I had roommates). One hundred square feet of fornicating possibilities, which sat as far across the compound from my pod as any one pod could sit. It's like they *wanted* it to be hard for us to have sex. Regardless, the fact of the matter was that there was no tiptoeing around corners or sneaking down hallways if I wanted to get my hands on Libra's top-secret briefs, if you know what I mean. (Sex. I mean sex.) I had to cover a good chunk of open ground any time I went to or from our respective pods, which violated my soldier's sense of tactical decency, if I'm being honest. The best time to "infil" was typically at lunch, when I could come up with a semi-decent explanation for why I needed to head over in that direction.

Now, I don't want to give anyone a false impression here. While Libra and I did have full, unlawful carnal knowledge of each other countless times over the course of my deployment, and despite the fact that I am widely regarded in military circles as a generous and passionate lover with above-average stamina—I *regularly* satisfied Libra for two, three, sometimes even four minutes at a stretch—neither she nor I flaunted our exploits or got lost in the passion. We kept things on as much of the DL as possible, which didn't turn out to be all that much in the end, because we'd regularly leave the chow hall together after dinner. Then on the nights when I didn't have work the next day, I'd stay over and come out of her pod the next morning to find six people standing there in the hall. That was not being very *covert*.

Fortunately, no one ever said anything. They just stared and went on about their day. For the most part, everyone was pretty cool about it, actually. The salty old guys were oblivious, deployed elsewhere, or so despised by everyone else that the enemies of my enemy became my friends. It helped that I was good at my job, and I got along with everyone pretty well, too. If I'd been a dickhead, someone would have found the perfect opportunity to out us and bring the whole thing crumbling down.

That opportunity, had someone chosen to accept it, arrived on Halloween, when I decided to dress up for the base Halloween party as Jessica Simpson's version of Daisy Duke from the *Dukes of Hazzard* movie. Since I didn't have to work the next day, I went all-out. I had the wig, the cut-off jorts, the high heels, even the makeup. *Yeah*. Full lipstick, rouge, mascara, the whole nine. When I tell this story to other military people who know me, the part that shocks them the most isn't the cross-dressing, it's that the ██ organized a Halloween party.

The hardest part wasn't even getting up the nerve to do it; the hard part was the physical act of getting dressed as a woman in a 100-square-foot room with no mirror. As a guy, you can get dressed and shave 90 percent of your face in total darkness in under five minutes. Grown women, who have been dressing themselves, doing their hair, and applying makeup for years, still need like six different mirrors of varying shapes, sizes, and magnification just to be squared away enough to leave the house. Not by choice, either. It's just what you have to do as a woman. You can't risk going out in public all ratchet and uncoordinated. Men won't care, but other women will eat you alive—trust me, I know, I was about to be a woman for eight hours, that kind of makes me an expert.

I recognize now that the prospect of a jacked six-foot-two dude rolling into a party in high heels and makeup is frightening even under ideal conditions, but I had no idea then just how terrifying it would be if that dude had to do a poor man's version of what a woman has to do every day *and* he couldn't see himself as he tried to do it.

When I walked into the party, the reaction was split down the middle: Half the people were insanely impressed with my outfit, the other half looked at me like someone just let John Wayne Gacy into a Boy Scouts meeting. Go big or go home, I say. To Libra's credit, she thought my costume was hilarious, which meant only one thing to me: It was time to drink.

Yeah, so here's the thing about that: Getting drunk and going back to Libra's pod while dressed as a woman left me in a very compromising position the next day. When I finally woke up, it was well into the afternoon, and Libra was at work because she was a mature adult who could handle her shit. With nowhere in particular I needed to be, I casually rolled over and grabbed some water from the side of the bed to start beating back the hangover that was fortifying its position behind my eyeballs. As I took a big, long, lukewarm drink, I spotted my Daisy Dukes wadded up on the floor, sitting there all by themselves, eye-fucking me. I could hear them in my mind, taunting me: *Howdy there, stranger, y'all fixin' to mosey on out of these parts? Fine and dandy . . . reckon it'll be just you and me, huh?*

Motherfucker. I had no clothes of my own to change into. I wasn't actually embarrassed about owning the Halloween party, but I also couldn't immediately recall what I said or did when I was there. In those few seconds of doubt, as I wrestled with the fact that I had nothing else to wear, a wave of terror washed over me. I was going to have to throw this outfit back on in order to leave. Talk about the ultimate walk of shame.

Somehow, peeking around corners and clutching my ill-fitting pair of high heels (which I refused to put back on), I made it to the front of Libra's building without being seen. It was a miracle that I knew would not be replicated. As soon as I stepped outside, someone spotted me. I instinctively pressed my body against the side of the building to make myself a smaller target, but it was no use. Fortunately the guy who saw me was a friend. I waved and tried to whisper-yell at him to come over. At first he wouldn't, because it's hard to walk when you're doubled over laughing, but eventually the desperation in my eyes and the mascara running down my face convinced him to do a little recon. With the appropriate amount of begging, he radioed my buddy to bring some of my clothes to Libra's room and end my panicked misery.

All in all, the ordeal lasted maybe five minutes, but it was the longest five minutes of my life. Like running a mile while holding your breath. It brought my respect for women to a whole new level. You not only birth us and raise us, but you put in so much effort to look like a slutty nurse, all for our benefit, and when it works, the next day we make you find your own way back to the ER *stat*. I finally understood what every single shacker who has ghosted from my house at 8 A.M. has gone through. It's fucking miserable. To you fine women, I'd like to say that I'm sorry.

When I got back to my room I grabbed an old towel and scrubbed off my makeup. Then I checked my email. My eyes lit up in horror when I saw this message at the top of my inbox:

> *Hey, you're not going to believe this, but I just got orders to go on a surprise trip to your site. How crazy is that? See you in a week!*
>
> ~*XOXO*
> *Scorpio*

Fuuuuuuuuuuuuuuuckkkkkkkk. I forgot about the biggest problem of them all when it came to hooking up with Libra: I was kinda sorta already seeing this other girl from another ▮▮▮▮. Her name was ▮▮▮▮ but in keeping with the astrological theme, I'll call her Scorpio since that is the name of the giant stinging, snapping, stabbing beast that the earth goddess Gaia sent to kill Orion the Hunter when he started to think he was hot shit. Scorpio and I were just talking and we'd only messed around a few times *and we had never had the talk* so there was no way she could possibly think we were, like, "together."

But still . . . out of all the ▮▮▮▮▮▮▮▮, in all the world, she had to get sent to mine. I was in full-blown panic mode. The place was already small enough, but it just so happened that on the ███ she was coming from, Scorpio worked in the same exact office doing the same exact job that Libra did on this one. There was no way they wouldn't be working together. I had a better shot of contracting polio than getting through two days without them finding out that they were the bread in a Mat sandwich.

The week before Scorpio arrived, my head was swimming with possibilities. What should I do? What do I say when she gets here? To either of them. By this point in the trip, I was really into Libra and I thought there might be a chance we could date for real back stateside. I didn't want Libra to find out that I had been semi-dating a girl before I met her and that I hadn't been totally clear and forthright from the beginning. With my job history I had been used to pulling the slow fade or just the straight-up Houdini. This crossing of streams was new to me, and I didn't want to get twisted up in the middle of it and come out seeming like an undateable asshole.

The way I looked at it, I had three options.

Option Number One: "Lie, Deny, Counter-Accuse"

We've all done this one. It usually starts with phrases like "I don't even know her" or "She's making this up." This portion is the *lie*. That's followed up by "I didn't fuck her" and "I promise on a stack of bibles," which is the *denial*. The masterstroke, the third leg on this tripod of deflection, is the *counter-accusation*, where you flip the script and project all your guilt onto her. "Why are you so mad right now? Why are you yelling? I bet because you're fucking somebody and you feel guilty about it. Tell me I'm wrong." When you're stuck on a ███ ████████████ sleeping in ten-by-ten rooms, "Lie, Deny, Counter-Accuse" doesn't work.

Option Number Two: Radical Transparency

When Scorpio arrives, at the first available opportunity, I could sit down with both of them, come completely clean, and let the chips fall where they may. We're all rational adults with professional jobs here. We can talk this out in a sensible manner, right?

In the movies, this is how the really good threesomes start. I hope you don't think I did that. Not a goddamn prayer in this world or the afterlife would I think for one second about trying to get away with that.

Option Number Three: Pass Her Off to a Friend

I know, I'm a terrible person for even thinking that was an option. That's just too fucked up. But do me a favor, before you sit in judgment, close your eyes and pretend for a second that this is a storyline in one of those old Choose Your Own Adventure books. Now, take a deep breath and go ahead and choose this adventure, because that is exactly what I did.

When Scorpio arrived, things went from zero to awkward *real* quick. Instead of falling back on my training and pushing forward to clear through the objective, I hung back, kept my head down, and tried to avoid her as much as possible. It worked about as well as hiding from a drunk relative at Christmas. Pray as hard as you want, they're not going away. Out of the gate, Scorpio was pretty aggressive about wanting to get romantic. It wasn't immediately obvious to me if she was trying to rekindle the flame or if it was just her loins that were on fire, but I didn't want to find out. As soon as I found the chance, I introduced her to my buddy, the same guy who had brought me my clothes the morning after my Jessica Simpson Halloween triumph.

Trying to be subtle, I invited a few people over to my pod, including Scorpio and my buddy, at a time when I knew Libra would be working. I would arrange it so he and Scorpio had time to interact, and then I would choose a moment to slip away, basically "gifting" her to him. (Jesus, even typing that sentence feels gross.) My buddy was definitely into her, and I could tell that she at least wasn't disgusted by him, but deep down I also knew that there was no way I was getting out of this cleanly. Libra or Scorpio were going to hate me; there was no way around it. To be honest, I was into Libra enough that I was fine with Scorpio hating me. I just had to figure out how to tell them both in a way that hurt them the least (and that made sure Libra didn't kick me to the curb).

After much thought, I decided to go to Libra first and tell her about me and Scorpio. Surprisingly, she was pretty cool about it and appreciated my honesty. Then I told Scorpio about Libra, which went less well. Though I guess that depends on your perspective and experience. A few days later, as I was passing Scorpio's room, I bumped into my buddy walking out. I could have been pissed, the way I was when I found out Awful Person was still fucking her ex-boyfriend, but instead I was psyched. The dribble handoff had worked. I went in for the single-arm bro shake-hug. And he ducked it. Scorpio had Vader'd him with her love force and turned him against me. Things were strained between him and me after that, because let's be honest, how can you maintain the same depth of friendship with the guy who, in your mind, fucked and chucked the new girl you're in love with? I understood, and I let it go.

Thankfully, this particular deployment was almost over, so I was able to give them their space and not have to worry about seeing them very often. If this had all gone down a couple months earlier, who knows where it could have ended. That combination of uncertainty and inevitability is exactly why my contracting agency frowned upon fraternizing with the ▮▮▮▮. Over a long enough time horizon, it's going to end, and most likely it will end poorly.

With just a few days left before I rotated home, I remember sitting on my twin bed in my shitty little room in the middle of ▮▮▮, having a couple drinks by myself, and scrolling through a digital swampland of complainers on Facebook. *My flight is delayed! My latte is cold! WTF, I can't get a latte on this flight?!* As I perused this pathetic chorus of first-world whining, all I could think about was my brother Alan. Not all the things he'd been through to beat cancer and serve his country, but rather all the things he *never said or did* as he got down to business and got himself squared away. He never complained, he never made excuses, he never asked for pity or for a break. He just did his job. His calmness and deliberation and fortitude became subtle forms of inspiration for me from the day he got the news—of his diagnosis, of the planes hitting the building, of the long road ahead for him.

As I thought about my brother and Brehm and Barraza and other guys we'd lost during deployments, everything that got me to where I was in that moment, I just remember how pissed I was at all those Facebook people. To defuse some of my spite, I picked up my guitar and started strumming some chords, talking to them out loud through my computer screen, *you fuckers and your champagne problems, everyone's got 'em.* Before I knew it, two hours had passed and I'd written and recorded a song that would become my first YouTube video: "Champagne Facebook Problems." Little did I know it would change my life forever.

Chapter 16

Hey, Aren't You That Dude?

I didn't publish "Champagne Facebook Problems" right away. I sat on it for a few days as I considered what to do with it. I'd used GarageBand to record the audio tracks and the camera on my MacBook to record the video, so I wasn't exactly psyched with the production quality. And on a more basic level, the whole thing felt kind of embarrassing. I mean, sure, I've always loved playing music and writing songs, but I'm a former Ranger and was working as ███████████. Calling attention to yourself like this isn't something you do unless you're a contestant on *The Voice* or you're a Navy SEAL. #sickburn

Still, something about the process of coming up with an idea and producing a piece of content with a message that I thought more people needed to hear tapped into a feeling that was bigger than my macho insecurity—a reservoir of creativity within me that I'd unwittingly spent the previous ten years covering up with muscles, tattoos, body armor, and guns. All it took was the crushing boredom of private military contracting to smash a crack in that façade and allow some of the creativity to vent.

For all of it to *fully* vent, however, my creation had to reach more than an audience of me, so I hit "publish" and told a few buddies about it to get the ball rolling. Even at this early stage, I knew I had more videos in me, but if nobody wanted to watch them, I wasn't going to waste my time. Fortunately, by telling my friends, who told their friends, "Champagne Facebook Problems" got a few thousand views and I got a few hundred subscribers to my YouTube channel, which I called "MBest11x," in the first couple weeks. In retrospect, that's not a lot, but when you're first starting out, anything more than nothing feels pretty amazing. As the investor Peter Thiel says, the hardest part of any creative or entrepreneurial endeavor is going from zero to one.

Plus, on a personal level, seeing the likes and the subscriptions and the comments tally up, however small, was actually really rewarding. And not in the social media validation whore kind of way either, you judgy bitches. More to the extent that something I had created was resonating with an audience that wasn't my classmates or close friends. In high school, with Blind Story, people liked us but we didn't have "fans." Nobody bought any CDs or merch (not that we had any). Like with most high school bands, half of the admiration we received was from people who just thought it was cool that they knew somebody who owned a microphone. The response to "Champagne Facebook Problems," that was a different beast, and I wanted to tame it. So for the next year and a half, I treated my time off like a daddy's girl in a freshman dorm: All I did was experiment.

I made a video called "Exploding Bear!!" using 30-plus cases of ammo, a giant pink teddy bear, and some Tannerite, all or some of which (depending on who from Battalion is reading this right now) I purchased drunk online one night, flush with all that contractor money.

I did a video sitting at a desk talking straight to the camera called "How to Pick Up Chicks." (Short answer: Lift with your legs.) Then I moved away from talking to the camera and I did a sketch about all the dumb shit guys do, just to see how a video might turn out if I scripted it and tried to act a little bit. That video was (geniusly) titled "Dumb Shit Guys Do," and it was the first one I'd done that I was actually proud of. The editing was better, the ideas were sharper, I added title graphics and outro music with a "Subscribe" tag at the end that made it seem like I knew what the fuck I was doing, and I was able to incorporate some military-specific material into other pop culture stuff that made the video even more relevant to the people I already knew would be my core fan base: military dudes and dudettes.

It was good enough, I thought, to warrant reaching out to a couple of the bigger online military communities to see if they'd share it. With each video I made, my audience was growing, and the messages I was getting were more enthusiastic, so clearly I was doing something right. One of the first places I tried was a large general-interest military page on Facebook run by an active-duty Air Force guy named Jarred Taylor. I sent him a message along with links to my other videos to show him who I was and what kind of content I was capable of making. Fairly certain he had received tons of requests like this, I didn't think he would reply. I was shocked when I got a message back two minutes later. It was terse and simple: "Can we talk? Here's my number."

I was confused. What did he want to talk about? Are you gonna share the video or not? Yes or no? The next day, I dialed Jarred's number, not really sure why I was doing it. He picked up right away.

"Dude, I've been searching for someone like you for a long time," he said, virtually unprompted. "I love your videos, and I think you have a really great presence. I can help you."

"How so?" I asked. I was unsure what "help" meant in the context of YouTube videos. Plus, isn't this how aspiring models end up dead in a river? Some predator sees potential in them and uses a camera to lure them into a van that locks from the outside?

"I own a video and graphics company," Jarred continued. "I've been doing production for the last ten years on my own. Everything from music videos and commercials to sketches like yours. A bunch for people in the tactical space. I think I have some contacts that could help us."

Help us with what?

"Look, I would love for you to come down to El Paso where I live so we can shoot a bunch of stuff. We need to get you better production."

"What do you mean?" I was skeptical but excited.

"I'm talking about making people think you are already a suc-cessful personality. *A brand.* Come down to Texas and we can talk more. I'll shoot everything when you're here."

"Shit, I can't. I'm deploying in like a week."

"Okay, no problem, just come down when you get back."

After we hung up the phone and I replayed the conversation in my head, I found one thing especially remarkable about it. In all of his sentences, Jarred used the word "we" when describing what he wanted to do. It's like we were already partners on something that didn't even exist yet. I wasn't a *personality.* I was just Mat. I was a guy who liked playing music and blowing shit up who hap-pened to have a lot of time on his hands.

We started talking on the phone and messaging each other every day after that while I was deployed to Iraq. It was like we were high school sweethearts, excited about making plans for the fu-ture together. We knew each other's work and sleep schedules. He even FaceTimed me in the shower one day. I could hear his wife yelling at him.

"Are you really FaceTiming a dude in the shower that you've never met?!"

"Don't worry, Mrs. Taylor!" I shouted through the FaceTime screen. "There are no dick and balls in the frame!"

Two days after I got home from Iraq, I flew down to El Paso and stayed with Jarred for five days. When I landed, he picked me up from the airport and even came inside to baggage claim to greet me like a lady. On the drive back to his house, he pointed out the restaurants he thought I'd like and the gyms he thought would suit my needs.

"A bunch of these places are for sale," he said, pointing to differ-ent houses in a residential neighborhood. "You can rent them too. I know the dude who rents them out."

He was talking like a real estate agent welcoming a new family to the neighborhood, as if I was moving there or something. I just nodded as we turned in to his driveway. Wait, this was *his* neigh-borhood? Who was this crazy bastard?

Jarred and his house had a lot in common. They were good-sized, they looked nice and well maintained on the outside, but on the inside they were a total fucking nuthouse. The living room had no furniture and no TV, just band equipment and amplifiers. The first room he showed me was a spare bedroom that was decked out with more editing gear than a local TV station.

"Pretty cool, huh? I told you, I got everything down here," he said.

"Yeah, man, this is awesome. Where are your wife and daughter?"

"They're around somewhere, I don't know. Probably out getting us food or something."

"And she's cool with you having a small concert venue in your living room? You don't even have a couch."

"No, we do. It's out in the garage," he said in a matter-of-fact way, as if this was a completely normal thing.

"Why is it out in the garage?"

"I spend most of my time out there." That was the least surprising thing I had learned since touching down in El Paso. "Come on, I'll show you. Let's shoot some shit."

"Wait, where am I sleeping?"

"I got a room for you."

Jarred walked me down the hall to a spare bedroom that resembled something out of a porn shoot for *Black Ops Back Door Bonanza*. It was completely bare except for a queen-sized bed and about a dozen AR-15s on the floor. I looked at the mini-arsenal lying there thinking, *Those muzzle brakes have definitely been inside more than just a tactical carrying case.* I dropped my bag and Jarred took me out to the garage. What the fuck had I gotten myself into?

As soon as he hit the lights, I knew exactly what I had gotten into: production gold. He basically had a professional photography studio out there. I'm talking five-point light kits, 5D cameras, props, and every kind of backdrop you could imagine, from simple pastels to green screens. This motherfucker wasn't kidding when he said he had all the necessary production gear. He had *every-*

thing. It was incredible. He turned on one of the light kits and focused a camera on a backdrop.

"All right," he said, "let's get started."

Within a matter of days after leaving El Paso, my Facebook page and YouTube channel began growing exponentially within the military community. Initially, my newfound popularity wasn't a problem, because I was still able to float under the radar when I was deployed. Except for my first two trips as a contractor, I wasn't really around any military. I worked with the same small team of contractors at the same small ██, which housed contractors and ██████████████████, with no active-duty military present except for the occasional ██ team that would swing through. Everyone there already knew me and had seen my earlier videos, so none of this stuff was new to them. In this little bubble of ours, I was still just the guy who was the head of security and who would sit around the fire with them after work like one of the guys, drinking a beer, bullshitting about life. The only difference, now, was that I would float possible sketch ideas by them and write down the funny shit they said. In a way, they were invested in my videos, so they weren't surprised each time one posted.

The reason my team members and I consistently worked together for nearly four years straight was that we were always on the same deployment cycle. But by early 2014, when things really started to kick off with the videos, I had to start changing up my deployment schedule to take advantage of opportunities to film and promote and do other business-related things. The first time I decided to delay one of my deployments and take extra time off, it was to go to the SHOT Show hosted by the National Shooting Sports Foundation in Las Vegas to promote my channel MBest11x. This pushed my next deployment to the following slot in the rotation, which meant that my normal assignment to Iraq would no longer be open and I would have to deploy to another theater. In this instance, Afghanistan. Specifically, I'd be detailed to "The

Flagpole," which is where NATO and all the military brass and a shit-ton of enlisted dudes were garrisoned. Fine by me, no big deal. To my mind, that just meant it would be easier to blend in. Oh Mat, you beautiful idiot.

First day: "Hey, aren't you that dude from YouTube?"

"Uh, yeah."

The guy slugged me hard on the shoulder. "Holy shit! I knew it was you! Your videos are fucking hilarious, man! Keep up the good work!"

"Thanks, man."

He smiled and walked off. I stood there stunned for a minute. SHOT Show aside, I had never been recognized for something other than what I did while I was in uniform or who I was caught with when I was stripped naked out of it. It was one thing to sit there and watch the YouTube subscriber numbers and Facebook friends grow into the thousands, but it was something else altogether to put a face to one of those numbers. It was surreal.

With each successive deployment, I met more and more people who seemed to already know who I was and thought what we were doing was cool. At one base, even the new interpreter assigned to me by the Afghan government knew who I was. I mean, this dude spent the first two hours of our training eye-fucking me so hard that I didn't know if he was an insurgent or in love.

"Is there an issue, Sparky?" I finally asked.

"No sir, but are you the American that does the guns and bikinis?"

"What?"

"You know. The American who knows how to pick up women on YouTube?"

Oh fuck, he was talking about my video, "How to Pick Up Chicks."

"Ha, I've heard I look like him."

"I knew it! The guns and the tits that I like. The freedom blanket! This is great!"

"All right, dude, keep your voice down. And let's not be telling the guard force about this, okay?"

"Yes, sir. I play it cool. Like your videos."

My team member just threw his gloves down and started laughing.

"Really, Mat? Are you fucking kidding me?" he chuckled.

As my notoriety continued to grow on these military installations, it became abundantly clear that I needed to find a way to lower my profile when I was deployed. In a place where secrecy and security are the Adam and Eve of standard operating procedures, I wasn't doing anyone any favors by drawing attention to myself like a public figure. I just wanted to fly under the radar and do my job.

One day I was at the chow hall and I got approached by a dude who wanted a picture. Of course, that's totally cool. I'm still flattered that people want to put in the effort to capture their interaction with me. So I get up, the dude pulls out his phone, and we take the picture. No big deal. *Up, snap, handshake, down.* It's like a fame burpee. I didn't think anything more about it until later that night when I went back to my room and opened my computer. Right there on Facebook, under the "Notifications" tab, I saw that someone had tagged me in a photo. It was the guy from earlier, of course. I clicked on the notification and read the caption:

In Kabul, hanging out with Mat Best!

Now it was my turn to sound like my team leader. I messaged the guy right away:

Really bro? Are you fucking kidding me? We've got beards, working a secret job, and you just told people where we are. You can't tag my name and our location in a fucking picture on Facebook!

Unbelievable. This isn't the Teen Choice Awards. I get it, the competition for "Choice Hissy Fit" is always a battle, but it's not an *actual* war zone like the place where we were living and working.

If this was any indication, it was only a matter of time before innocent pictures like this one began to jeopardize OPSEC, PER-SEC, InfoSec, triple sec, every other "Sec" you could think of. From that point forward on this deployment I made the executive decision to spend less time in the chow hall and start locking myself in my room after work. It sucked, and I hated to think that all these great guys who liked what we were doing might feel like I was big-timing them. But the less attention I attracted, the better off we all would be.

The one that really put it over the top for me, though, was my second-to-last deployment as a contractor, when I ran into the two highest-ranking members of 2nd Ranger Battalion—my former unit—in the chow hall on a base in Afghanistan. They were there networking with some of our personnel who they worked closely with on various operations. When I saw that they were all done eating, I went over to introduce myself. I barely got two words in before one of them made it clear he knew who I was.

"Keep doing great things," he said as he shook my hand. "You're a 2/75 guy, is that right?"

"Yeah, roger that, Sergeant Major."

"My son's a big fan," one of the officers said. "Can we take a picture?"

Can we take a picture? You're the brass of 2/75. You can take my anal virginity if you think it'll help. Obviously I didn't tell him that, since he already knew, I just stood next to him and put on my best "this isn't totally awesome" face. Knowing these pics would be in the hands of a hard-ass Ranger, I didn't have to worry about them ending up fucking geotagged on Facebook, so we whipped out our phones and snapped away right there in the chow hall.

When we were done, I ran back to my room and immediately texted Jarred to tell him what had happened, because, make no mistake, this was a big deal. When you're active duty, you never see the battalion brass unless someone fucks up or something really bad happens. In all my time in the 2/75, I don't think I ever materially engaged with my command sergeant major or a battalion officer. And if I did, I definitely didn't do it as a peer, like I just had as a contractor.

But more importantly, the command sergeant major's words made it clear to me that what we were doing with these videos wasn't just goofy and fun. It was important and had value to the community. It always feels good to make people laugh, but when it reached people in that environment, where there isn't a whole lot to laugh about, it gave everything we were doing a sense of deeper purpose. It also confirmed for me something I would barely allow myself to think and would never verbalize to others: I might actually be able to do this full-time, for a living. It was scary and liberating at the same time. Up until then, my primary concern wasn't whether the video stuff could be successful; it was whether I was gradually fucking up both possible career paths—contractor and whatever this was—by splitting my time and attention between them.

I was about to find out.

Chapter 17

Shirts & Shots & Shows & Service

I will be the first to admit that for most of my adult life, if it didn't involve weapons, war, or women, I had no fucking clue what I was doing. I was just faking it until, fingers crossed, I was making it. I was throwing shit at the wall hoping something would stick. Now that these videos were sticking, I started to think a little bigger about what they might be able to accomplish.

Jarred and I had already started to come up with all sorts of grand plans for the YouTube channel and the Facebook page, but it was about more than that. It was about building a platform to convey a larger message. The one thing I kept coming back to—an issue that had become really frustrating to me—was the way people in our society talk about veterans. All you ever heard about in the news or on TV shows were things like the destructiveness of PTSD or the crippling nature of survivor's guilt.

And while some veterans do suffer from those issues, if *Law & Order* did an episode where a soldier killed someone, it was never because he was an evil prick who *happened* to be in the military (the Marines, obviously), it was because he'd done a tour in Iraq and he saw his best friend die in an IED attack and it broke his brain and then he came home and everything was different and he couldn't sleep and it made it hard for him to hold down a job and then he got evicted from his apartment and then his girlfriend fucked his best friend and took his dog. *Blah blah blah blah blah*. Every veteran story was just this endless parade of horribles. What they failed to show, time and again, was my experience, which was the same as the experience of the hundreds of veterans I've known and served with who *loved* their time in the military and to this day view it as one of the most important, meaningful, *enjoyable* periods of their lives. No matter where you looked, there was no appetite for our stories anywhere. It felt like the forces that controlled the culture, that attempted to shape how we reckon with war and the warriors who fight it, had not built enough tolerance into the system, or put enough slack in the line, to accommodate the powerful notion that there are men and women out there who put their lives at risk to fight for others, to fight for an ideal, not because they had to but because they wanted to, they needed to. These were the forces that convinced civilians to thank us for our service on airport concourses all across America, in solemn, guilt-riddled tones, like we must have been compelled, reluctantly, to sacrifice our freedom, when in fact we had proactively exercised it to enlist and do something we loved.

As I continued to make videos, my goal was to speak to people like me. People who appreciated the gratitude but had no use for the pity; who did not need thanks for their service because they were more thankful for it than anyone could imagine. They were grateful for the chance to serve. I wanted to reflect their reality back to them so they would know that they weren't crazy *for not being crazy*. I also wanted any veterans and current active military who might be struggling to know that it was okay to laugh in the face of the horrors of war, that they could be proud of what they'd accomplished, and that there was at least one place online where no one would judge them either way. I wanted the world to know that veterans like me, who loved man shit like beards and whiskey and guns and hot chicks in American flag bikinis, weren't ticking time bombs waiting to explode. We were normal people who just so happened to have gone through some extraordinary experiences and come out the other side proud of our accomplishments, grateful for our brothers and sisters, and ready to apply all that experience to the next chapter of our lives in the civilian world . . . *and thrive.*

This was the mindset that Jarred and I shared as we set our minds to parlaying the popularity of our videos into an actual business. And we did it, principally, by listening to the voices of the very people we were trying to serve. It wasn't hard. With a fan base built largely from men aged 18 to 35 in the military community, believe me when I tell you that these dudes had fucking opinions. About everything: what they wanted, what they thought was funny, what they thought we were doing right or wrong, what they wanted more or less of. More importantly, they had ideas that were, by and large, way crazier and more fucked-up than anything Jarred and I could come up with on our own, by which I mean to say, *they were awesome.* So we started to aggregate and sort all their feedback, looking for patterns we could use to come up with sketch concepts, songs to parody, and business ideas to explore.

The first thing we launched was a T-shirt business. Military people have a tendency to wear cool lifestyle T-shirts, to work out in them, to have them on under their gear. If we made shirts with the same attitude and commitment to quality that we brought to making videos and used some of the more popular videos and what we would today call their "meme-worthy" content as inspiration for the designs and then used the videos to promote the shirts, we could turn some of this attention we were getting into a real business.

We called the company Article 15 Clothing, after the provision of the Uniform Code of Military Justice that governs getting in trouble but not *that bad* in trouble. Not "Did you order the Code Red?" court-martial trouble; more like fucking a ██ contractor, dressing up like Jessica Simpson, bringing a dude's head and shoulders back in a Glad-bag kind of trouble. As active-duty Air Force, it was Jarred's not-so-subtle way of saying "Fuck you, pay me" to the commanding officers whose stupid rules always made his job harder to do—I mean, to the extent that anything in the Air Force is actually difficult.

By any reasonable entrepreneurial standard, Article 15 Clothing achieved success right out of the gate—seven-figure sales in the first year—and with that success came expectations, the kind you cannot fail to meet if you intend to retain your customers and survive, let alone grow. We weren't just T-shirt peddlers, after all, we were also a mission-based business—like TOMS, except instead of "Sell a shoe, give a shoe" it was "Sell a shirt, give a freedom boner." Yes, on one level, people just wanted more. More T-shirts, more videos, more stuff. But on a deeper level, what we were hearing was a desire for a deeper connection.

I was getting messages on Facebook and emails in my inbox from all kinds of people, but especially veterans. Married guys with a gang of kids who'd been out of the service for a while, who missed the camaraderie of military life and saw their old Army buddies once a year if they were lucky. And they'd be like, *Bro! I love your stuff! Man, what I would give to be able to hang out and drink with you guys, even just for one night! Keep it up!*

Jarred and I and every member of the team we'd begun to assemble at Article 15 were getting these types of messages on a nearly daily basis. (I still get at least one per week, and I'm boring as fuck now.) It was flattering, and it was yet another indication that we were on to something in the name of good, but more than that it was the spark for two more ideas: If all these people wish they could drink and hang out with us, why don't we start a whiskey company and do a podcast? So eventually we did.

The whiskey company we called Leadslingers Spirits. The podcast we called *Drinkin' Bros*. Both are amazing, but only one was really a good idea. I won't say which, but word to the wise: If you hate having a fun, profitable, relatively frictionless professional life, the heavily regulated whiskey trade is the perfect business to get into. Brown liquor is great because it fucks you up nice and good. The whiskey business is awful because it fucks you up the butt without any lube and blames you for bleeding on its sheets. In contrast, for the one-hundredth episode of *Drinkin' Bros* we had two people have sex in front of us and we commentated it like a UFC fight. I'll leave it to you to choose which of these experiences you would prefer to be a part of.

In the middle of all this growth and entrepreneurial experimentation, we had our craziest idea yet. When I was overseas, we had this group chat on Facebook Messenger that we called "Kinetic Kill" where we bullshitted and brainstormed the way any company with a distributed workforce might. One night, we were kicking around sketch ideas when Jarred threw out something way more radical than a sketch concept: "Dude, we should make a fucking movie."

Okay, bro, yeah, we'll just make a movie. What the fuck are you talking about? Movies aren't sketches. They've got stories and actors. You need grips and shit. Movies cost a lot of money, even the low-budget ones. But the more Jarred talked and the more other guys on the chat chimed in, the more possible the idea seemed. More than a few fans had asked us to do something longer-form in the video space. There was definitely demand. And we could crowdfund it, just to be doubly sure that the demand was big enough. If only our moms donated to the campaign, we'd know it wasn't real. If we got close enough to our initial goal fairly quickly, then we'd know that success was really just a matter of getting the word out.

Pretty quickly we came to a consensus around an idea: It would be part comedy, part war epic, part zombie movie. The general gist was a group of buddies in the military save the world from a zombie apocalypse by bringing to bear all of their military training. Basically, it would be every military person's dream of slaying bodies in the name of survival (not that ISIS and zombies are too far apart in their thinking).

I floated the idea to the twenty or so American ███████████ I was working with overseas at the time who knew what I did on the side. They lost their minds. It was like Santa had come on the 4th of July with a bag full of guns and a team of Victoria's Secret elves intent on giving up their secret. For America, obviously. The support from my ███████████████████ was unequivocal, and their feedback followed the same general pattern, like a military Mad Libs:

Bro, that is so fucking [*amazing/awesome/ridiculous/cool*]. You
know what you absolutely HAVE to do? [*INSERT grotesque kill
or necrophilia sequence*]. Dude, can I be in your movie? Just like
as an extra or whatever. You don't have to pay me. I'll bring my
[*INSERT frighteningly large private weapons cache*].

Okay, so this was definitely the craziest idea we'd ever had, but
I was at least convinced now that it wasn't the stupidest. If we built
it, they would come. Also, they would watch it.

Just as quickly as the idea came together, so did everything else.
We partnered with another military-themed clothing company,
Ranger Up, to produce the film and create the Indiegogo campaign. We hired Ross Patterson as writer-director and worked with
him on the script, kicking around the most offensive jokes possible and the most elaborate kill sequences we knew we could pull
off, oftentimes over Messenger from thousands of miles away
while I was deployed. That insane chat thread, which still exists
archived somewhere, belongs in the Library of Congress, etched
into the wall of some kind of monument, or appended to a petition
at The Hague. I'm still not sure which.

I will spare you the details—no one wants to *read* about how a
movie happens, that's fucking boring—but the movie, called *Range
15* after the names of the two companies, was very successful as
far as self-financed independent films go. It was one of the largest
Indiegogo campaigns of all time. It rose to #1 and #2, respectively,
on the Amazon and iTunes charts for all movies the week of its
release. It featured William Shatner, Sean Astin, Keith David,
Danny Trejo, Marcus Luttrell, Randy Couture, and had the most
decorated military cast to ever appear in a movie. *Thanks, Clint,
Dakota, and Leroy. . . . I still owe you some beers!* It also spawned a
full AFE (Armed Forces Entertainment) tour of American military
installations in the summer of 2016 that, in a very real way,
changed my life because despite the outward success of Article 15
and Leadslingers and *Drinkin' Bros* and now the movie, internally
things weren't great.

———

Here's the thing about scaling a business: You have to hire people you can trust, or at least learn to trust, because they are going to be the ones you delegate entire segments of the business to handle. Having spent virtually my entire adult life in the military, the only people I really trusted were other people from the military. We look after our own. Whatever objective is placed in front of us, our goal is to conquer it. Together. Whoever Jarred and I were going to partner up with in those early days, I knew I wanted them to have served. I didn't care which branch, I just knew that I needed them to share our beliefs about service, sacrifice, and brotherhood. I didn't need them to have fought next to me in the trenches or anything like that, but they sure as shit better know what it's like to sleep in a hole or sit down in freezing swamp water at 0400.

I knew what this kind of veteran looked like when I saw them— I worked and lived with hundreds of them—but I had no idea where to find them in the civilian world, mostly because I was still working as a contractor as we launched the business, which meant that I was out of the country for months at a time. Fortunately we had Jarred, who pretty much knew everyone. Still does. I remember one time we randomly came up with a skit and needed girls for a last-minute shoot, so Jarred walked into a Mexican restaurant at 1 P.M. on a Tuesday and pulled out two waitresses who were in the middle of working the lunch shift to come out to his house and wear bikinis in a video. *For free.* Every guy has that friend or relative in his life who has the stones to do shit like this. Jarred was mine.

He knew a former Air Force guy who had become a graphic designer, and he hired him to make us a logo. He found another veteran who traded us three months of accounting work for an AR-15 with full mods, because freedom. He hired his old Air Force boss to run our website. We hired a close friend and former Ranger, Vincent Vargas, to assist in all things marketing. There were probably a hundred other things like that he pulled off that I didn't even know about while I went back and forth between El Paso and El Sandbox. I'm glad he did them, too, because almost without even realizing it, we stumbled ass-backward into a veteran-owned, veteran-run, veteran-supported business model.

This arrangement worked just fine for the first few years. Videos got made. T-shirts got shipped. Whiskey got drunk. Podcasts got recorded. But as our successes became more self-perpetuating—when we didn't have to hustle quite as hard to sell a thousand of the newest T-shirt as we had for the T-shirt before, or the T-shirt before that—I noticed that certain members of the team weren't carrying their weight. The little things were getting missed. Things that make a business more efficient and therefore more profitable. Things that, in the military, can be the difference between living and dying.

What made matters worse, because I was deployed constantly and I was out of the country more than half the time as a result, there were people on the team who thought that either I didn't care as much as they did or that I was doing less work than them. At best, especially as the company really started to grow, I was simply out of sight, out of mind. At worst, I was just the social media monkey out in front of the business, not one of the integral players behind the scenes also helping make the business go. I could handle the ego hit of that kind of whispery shit talk; it was when it was combined with a hypocritical lack of effort that I got pissed.

Things on that front really started coming into focus once I quit contracting in May 2015 and the movie started to heat up. I was back stateside now on a permanent basis. I was there, in the flesh, every day, participating in board meetings and brainstorming sessions, leading writing sessions on the movie with Ross, doing conference calls with the Ranger Up guys, filming with Jarred and developing our brand, both for the company and for the movie's Indiegogo page. All those naysaying shit talkers got a good long look at just how much work I did and how much energy I put into our business. And I, in contrast, got a courtside seat for their abject fuckery.

Still, I gave them all the benefit of the doubt and put my concerns on the back burner, because in the month between when I quit contracting and our Indiegogo campaign closed, we raised nearly $1.5 million. That was real fucking money, and we had to deliver. This shit had just gotten serious, and it demanded our best effort and complete focus. We spent the entire summer writing and casting and scouting locations, all on top of our normal business workload.

In October, we shot for an insanely hectic two weeks outside Los Angeles. The following June the movie exploded on its release, and shortly thereafter I found myself overseas with Jarred showing it to thousands of American servicemen and women.

The tour was one of the most humbling experiences of my life. Wherever we went, hundreds and sometimes thousands of soldiers lined up to come in and watch our movie, then afterward lined up all over again to say hi, take pictures, and share a moment. It had barely been a year since I'd been more or less where they were—deployed, armed, battle ready, surrounded by brothers and sisters. Now I was standing there in shorts and a T-shirt and flip-flops, selfishly worried about the loyalty of some of my own team back home, but also just as ready to shoot the shit with these guys as I was ready to go out and shoot the shit out of bad guys.

It was a complete mindfuck. There were days when I experienced a wider range of emotions than a bipolar *Bachelor* contestant. I was experiencing pride and envy and sorrow and excitement and nostalgia and hopefulness and a whole host of other feelings that are traditionally prohibited by either the man code or the Army Field Manual.

On one of our last nights of the tour, we were in Iraq doing a screening and a meet-and-greet at a small forward operating base. When the event was over, we got ferried back to the Green Zone in Baghdad in the back of a Black Hawk helicopter. It was late. The other guys in our group had quickly fallen asleep, and I found myself sitting at the edge of the open door staring out into the night as we raced a couple hundred feet over the hot desert of Iraq. A flood of emotion washed over me. I had been over these very same sands with Brehm and Barraza years earlier. I was sitting right where Barraza was when he too stared out into the Iraqi night while his team slept and prepped on the way to the target where he and Brehm would make the ultimate sacrifice.

Somewhere out beyond my field of vision, their legacy mixed with the sands we now flew over. They became part of the history of this place, just like the lessons they taught me as a private and an idiot kid became part of my character as the man only they had known, for certain, I was capable of growing into.

Their example relit a fire inside me in that moment, one that I knew I would need to use as both fuel and as a guiding light in dealing with shit back home. Shit that had to change. Because I wasn't a warfighter anymore. I wasn't just a veteran who happened to have a business. I was a *leader* in the business. I was an entrepreneur. And I had to start acting like it.

Months later, we were in Colorado for the taping of the one-hundredth episode of *Drinkin' Bros,* hanging out in the hotel suite where in a few hours two perfect strangers would bang in front of us (for the best podcast ever), and I officially reached my limits. Actually, I had reached my limits much earlier than that, but I needed this time to come to some important realizations before I could have the "Come to Jesus" talk I was prepared to give right then.

As the co-founder of veteran-owned, veteran-run businesses, I didn't want to accept that some of the people we had hired or partnered with couldn't cut it. That they weren't up to the challenges of entrepreneurship. Or worse, that they weren't upstanding partners. My denial was as much about my own judgment as it was about this romantic ideal of veterans that I'd allowed myself to get swept up in. What I realized was that, at least when it came to the guys who weren't pulling their weight or were talking shit, I had fetishized their veteran standing just like all those TV and movie producers who turned their veteran characters into puddles of PTSD. I had painted a picture of them as faultless heroes who could push further, work longer, and go harder than anyone else.

That was a mistake. Brehm and Barraza were not demigods. They were men. Men of uncommon courage and unimpeachable valor, but still just men. It was a disservice to them and the entire veteran community to paint their accomplishments as the product of something other than their own hard work and sacrifice. Something that anyone, if they set their mind to it, can achieve. Because the whole point of what we were trying to do, from the very beginning with our videos, was to show the world that veterans, at their core, are just people. They did not lack humanity because they chose to fight. They did not *lose* their humanity as a result of war. Nor did they turn into idols of worship. Just as civilians can be amazing or they can be assholes, so too can veterans. Their military service may have been the best experience of their lives, but it didn't redefine who they were in the fucking animal kingdom.

The veterans I was working with were still human beings, and if they stood any chance of getting back to normal life, like we said they could (and should), then I needed to start treating the veterans closest to me—my partners, my employees—the same way. The kid gloves had to come off. The standards of private-sector business needed to be applied. Everyone should get the same amount of rope. You could use it to climb up to the top of our growing organization, to swing to another opportunity nearby, or to hang yourself.

That process started in Colorado in the late fall of 2016. I stepped up to take the reins that I felt belonged to me and willingly assumed all the responsibilities that came with it. I challenged the others in the room to step up and do the same thing. Some did and some did not. Those who did strapped into a star-spangled rocket ship of entrepreneurial success. Those who didn't, well, that was their choice. You're allowed to have those in the civilian world—choices, I mean—and I had to be okay with theirs being different than mine.

No hard feelings, just hard goodbyes.

Chapter 18

By Veterans, For Veterans

It's a funny thing, business. If you look at the history of any successful company that did well in its early days but then one year later grew like a weed and took over the market share, the people who were there at the beginning will always point to some singular decision to explain the explosive growth. Sometimes it's diversifying product offerings, sometimes it's changing the branding or the messaging, sometimes it's pivoting the entire business, sometimes it's getting rid of one toxic person, and sometimes it's adding one amazing person. Even if the reality of what had changed was more complicated and multifaceted, people want to zero in on that one thing, almost like a creation myth.

If you ask me, meeting Evan Hafer is what changed the trajectory of our business and, really, the rest of my life.

Back in the second half of 2014, before the movie or the podcast or any of the cracks in the company had started to appear, I was over in Afghanistan on another contracting cycle when I began to get reports from friends back home that someone pretty high up in the ███████████████████ was asking around about me. It wasn't a casual ask, which happens all the time; to my buddies, this seemed like some kind of systematic inquiry. It was a little unsettling, because I couldn't tell if I was being investigated or being vetted for ████████████, and I didn't have

enough juice inside ███████ to chase it down and find out one way
or the other.

I did my best to put it out of my mind and focus on my job, and
eventually the rumor mill stopped, but still it nagged at me until
one day Jarred emailed and said that a former Green Beret named
Evan Hafer had reached out to us through the Article 15 Facebook
page about a potential business opportunity. Evan, like me, had
been contracting with ████████ for a while and was living in Salt
Lake City when he wasn't in ████████ running the training
████████████████████████.

This was the fucker who had been asking after me.

Evan had a small coffee company on the side, where he'd been
roasting beans for nearly a decade. He'd seen our videos, and he
liked what we were doing with our apparel company, and he
thought with the Christmas season coming up, maybe there was a
way we could do some kind of pro-veteran, cross-promotional
thing that would be fun and profitable for us and give his operation a lift in exposure.

It was an intriguing idea. There were only two problems: One, I
knew fuck all about coffee. To me, coffee was a caffeine-delivery
system, and that was it. I even tossed a couple ice cubes into my
coffee sometimes just so it would cool down faster and I could
deep-throat it quicker. (I now recognize this move as utterly bar-
baric and sacrilegious.) Two, I was half a world away, modeling
my best short-sleeved plaid shirts for the indigenous forces I was
in charge of, so I couldn't vet Evan the way he had vetted me.
Jarred would have to do it.

A couple days after we chatted on the phone with Evan so he
could tell us more about what he was thinking, Jarred jumped on
a plane and flew up to Salt Lake City. When he got there, what he
found was not a "coffee company" so much as a "roaster in Evan's
basement." And who he met was not "Evan Hafer" but rather the
human embodiment of Rocket Raccoon from *Guardians of the
Galaxy*. Short and deceptively vicious, Evan will just sit there and
stare at you while you dig yourself a hole, then laugh in your face
and shit on your dreams while you try to crawl your way out of it.

He's one of the smartest, wittiest, most hardworking, most put-together guys you'll ever meet, which is why underestimating him will almost always cost you your ass.

Of course I didn't know any of this at the time. All I knew was that he had an idea: He would do a five-hundred-bag run of a special coffee blend, we'd do a video promoting it, and then we'd all get together afterward and go skinny dipping drunk off our asses and hope that no one noodled each other. Oh, and we'd call it Freedom Roasters Coffee.

Jarred and I talked it over and we quickly said yes to the dress. The video became "Grinch vs. Operators." It went live Thanksgiving Day 2014. The coffee was called Dark Roasted Freedom. It sold out by the end of the following week.

I am not good at many things. I can shoot. I can play guitar. I can grow a douchey beard. With pretty much everything else, I bridge the talent gap with effort and enthusiasm. The only other thing I've ever been good at is judging character and recognizing opportunity.

Evan Hafer was a solid gold human being, and this military-oriented coffee thing was a *massive* opportunity. This needed to be more than just a one-off Black Friday cross-promotion. This "thing" needed to be a business. There is just something so social and bonding about sharing a great cup of coffee with your friends, with your brothers. Not to mention that I wouldn't have to reinvent T-shirt designs every month, so I could focus on giving back to the community I love. Which meant I needed to take a good hard look at the opportunity.

With the end of 2014 fast approaching, Evan, Jarred, and I were done looking. We were ready to commit. By Christmas, we had a name: Black Rifle Coffee Company. Evan came up with it when he was at the range one morning, and out in the parking lot he had his fully modded, fully blacked-out rifle laid out on the tailgate of his truck next to the traveling coffee setup he used for road brews. Black Rifle + Coffee + Company. Don't ever let anyone tell you that us Army folk can't be creative AF. A week later, on the first business day of the new year, Black Rifle Coffee Company was formed.

Black Rifle Coffee took off. By the middle of 2015, the company's growth curve looked like it had Peyronie's disease: It went hard up and to the right. Even more, I was loving all the stuff we were doing in terms of content creation, product design, and employing and helping veterans. It was incredibly fulfilling the way the company collaboratively came together and embodied all the beliefs to which we'd dedicated our lives: teamwork, effort, opportunity, commitment, sacrifice, and shooting people in the face (this time with high-caliber caffeine).

And on a personal level, I'd found a kindred spirit in Evan. He was like the grown-up private-sector version of Danny Fulton. His work ethic, business savvy, and commitment to the veteran community were unrivaled. His sense of pride in his work and his country, and his loyalty to friends and fellow veterans, made him someone to admire, and made us, dare I say, BFFs.

And yet, despite all the work that needed to be done to grow this and the other businesses, despite all the marketing and branding decisions that needed to be made and that I had slowly developed a knack for, I was *still* doing contracting work at a ridiculously high tempo. I'd be home for barely more than the minimum required downtime between cycles, and then I'd be out the door and on a plane. I wasn't disconnected from the team, don't misunderstand. When I wasn't at work, I was in my room, on my laptop, answering emails, writing business models, doing Skype calls, you name it. Whatever BRCC or Article 15 or Leadslingers work needed to get done, on my off hours I was doing it.

I probably didn't need to keep deploying, since the business was doing well enough that I could have drawn a salary somewhere in between the peanuts I made in the Army and what, before Article 15, felt like stupid money from ██████. That was more than enough to live on. But I didn't want to stop deploying. I told myself that it was because I loved what I was doing with the ██████ that I kept accepting rotation slots. The work was still exciting and meaningful. I was working with good people doing important stuff. But I would be lying if I didn't say that all those messages we were get-

ting from fans kind of scared the shit out of me. They were express-
ing my worst fears. I had transitioned out of the military once
before, and re-entry had been really rough. I was worried that
quitting contracting would lead to the same outcome. Although I
felt that I had created a fairly good support system back home and
had found real purpose and camaraderie with Jarred and Evan
and the growing team at Article 15 and Black Rifle, I was still worried about giving up the real rifle. I was afraid of missing *that* kind
of team. Missing out on *that* kind of mission. Missing all the jokes,
all the shared experiences that I thought you can only get with others who are in harm's way, going through the same exact thing
you're going through. You have to realize: At twenty-eight years
old, I had dedicated nearly a decade of my life to service, and I
truly did love it. And while I recognized at the time that the way
I was hanging on to all of this was getting ridiculous, letting it
go wasn't so simple, especially when you were getting dozens of
messages every week basically confirming that life after service
could be this lonely, directionless march toward nothing, devoid
of meaning and camaraderie, where the only things you can count
on are the regretful voice in your head and then, finally, death.

(If you're reading this, Hallmark, I'm way ahead of you. I'm already working on a full line of Valentine's Day cards.)

Of course, I had yet to fully face the reality of my mindset, and
instead I rationalized my continuing deployment as a necessity for
the business. I was a prominent figure in military culture now.
Enlisted men and women looked up to me as an example of what
is possible for them after the military. They looked forward to the
crazy content we produced as a way to cope until their time came.
And since much of that crazy content was inspired by the men and
women I worked with on overseas installations, I couldn't just *not*
be there with and for them.

Jesus, I sound full of myself. Specifically, full of my own dick
and balls. How I can still stand up straight after all those years of
contorting myself to suck myself off, I have no idea. Moving on.

———

In early 2015, I finished a deployment that included the closest call I ever had as a contractor. It wasn't any kind of direct engagement like I'd had back in my battalion days. The closest, scariest calls never are. This was more like one of those "but for a totally unlikely, totally lucky series of small events, I'd be in a million pieces all over the desert right now" scenarios. I never saw the threat. The threat never saw me. But we were on a 100 percent collision course, and the only thing that saved me were those lucky, random intervening events.

For some reason, that got to me. I wasn't rattled, I was just frustrated with myself. *What the fuck am I doing? I am going to die out here, with everything good I've got going on back home, and I'm not even gonna see it coming. Why? Fuck this shit.*

One afternoon that spring, we found ourselves at a ranch just outside of El Paso owned by some kind of world-renowned horse-shoer who was raising horses and bulls. Why we were there, I still have no idea. There was some kind of business rationale, I assume. In our infinite wisdom, we figured why not take this opportunity to test drive Jarred's new drone camera while I attempted a skill I'd never tried before: maneuvering a temperamental 2,200-pound beast around a meadow with a series of subtle hand and foot gestures. The horse, however, was not so great at handling that drone, which sounded like a massive swarm of angry bees as it flew directly over our heads. I tried to pull back on the reins to settle her down (apparently this is not the right move). She was intent on getting me the fuck off her back, so she ducked her head and front legs and then reared back to fling me out of the saddle like I was a sack of shit in a trebuchet. I hit the ground *hard*. I broke my arm, nearly exploded my knee, and smashed my face. *My beautiful, beautiful face!*

Wanna guess what my first thought was as I rode to the hospital to get myself un-Humpty-Dumpty'd? Whether I would be able to make my next contracting rotation. I was supposed to be back at the qualification school in four days for training and to get recertified. I called my contracting agency.

"Hey, just so you know, I just took a bad spill. My knee's fucked, my arm's broken, and I need stitches."

"Omigosh, Mat. Are you okay?" said the woman from the contracting office.

"Yeah, yeah. So if I can shoot with one hand, can I still come?" There was a long pause.

"Jesus, Mat, worry about your health and safety!" she finally said.

"No, I know," I replied, briefly registering that what I had just asked was certifiable. "But can I still go if I only have one arm?"

At the time it didn't seem like too crazy of an ask (at least to me it didn't). It was my left hand that was hurt, and I'm naturally right-handed, so technically I still had my dominant side. If the hand was fractured, I figured I could just wrap it and go through the qualification course like that. NFL linemen do that all the time when they suffer a hand fracture. Jason Pierre-Paul blew half the fingers off one hand with fireworks, and he still played! I wasn't trying to be a macho tough guy. I really didn't want to miss this opportunity, because if you miss training one time you can get hard-pressed out of a job, and that was what I was worried about.

The people at the ███ were cool about it, and they didn't make me feel like a crazy person for asking if I could still come. They just said that the next job date was eight weeks out, and with how long it takes for a bone to heal, especially if you have to get pins put in, and then have the cast removed, and maybe go through rehab after that, it wasn't going to work. I would have cut my goddamn cast off if that was all there was to it, but that clearly wasn't the case here, so I postponed my recertification.

When my business partners found out that I'd broken my hand and my face and it had put me out of commission, they were happy, those fuckers. It meant that I would be stateside for an indefinite period of time, during which I could dedicate all of my focus to our businesses, particularly Black Rifle Coffee, which was beginning to catch massive steam.

Slowly, everything began to change. Every day I was more excited about all the stuff we were doing. Making videos and selling quality products to quality people is actually a lot of fun. And making money not dodging bullets is funner. Yes, *funner* is a word.

A few weeks later, we were in North Carolina for a big bar event at Fort Bragg to promote Leadslingers Spirits. The place was packed with active-duty military, guys from Bragg, guys from Article 15 and Ranger Up who were just then starting to work together on *Range 15*, veterans from all over the region, and assorted people from various parts of the government, including these two guys who introduced themselves by name and not by profession. After a few minutes our conversation went from fanboy to full bro, and they let it slip that they were actually instructors at the qualification course where I was scheduled to be in four days' time to recertify in preparation for my next contracting gig.

Yep, I was going back. But that's not what you should be focused on right now. You should be worried about the same thing I was: the people who were about to critique my professional skills, grade me, and make an official determination about whether I was still fit to do my job as an "operative" were *fans*. This was incredibly disconcerting, because it could go one of two ways, and neither of them was very good. They could treat me like a VIP and take it easy on me, or they could have super-high expectations that bordered on hard-ass one-upmanship and try to teach the Internet dude a lesson. In either case, it would have been much better to be anonymous.

I had been dealing with being recognized overseas for a while. The incidents had increased over time, but rarely did they get too egregious or uncomfortable. This was the first time that my personal life and my professional life had blended and fused so completely. I did not like it. Instantly, I lost interest in going back for recertification or even deploying at all. People could legitimately get hurt if this kind of fuckery were allowed to take place, and I hated that I might play a part in that. It was tremendously upsetting to me.

I spent the rest of the night drinking until I couldn't feel my feelings anymore. The next morning, Jarred and I nursed our hangovers over a batch of mimosas at some shitty restaurant. I vented to him.

"I honestly don't know how to manage this, Jarred."

"Fuck it, quit." You can always count on Jarred for the nuanced approach.

"It's not that easy," I said, and then I laid out all my reasons (translation: excuses) for staying in. Then we walked through all the *actual* reasons why quitting wasn't just easy but the sensible thing to do. I was ready, but there was still a Darby Phase river of bullshit to wade through.

The biggest bit of all wasn't actually the fear of nothingness or misery that, to this point, I'd used to rationalize staying in. It was this lingering fear I'd had since my fifth deployment—the one in Balad, with the crazy operational tempo; with Wendy Peffercorn; with the pool and the Taco Bell; with my Ranger buddies like Trey Bullock and Danny Fulton; with periods of true Rambo-esque greatness interrupted by moments of hardship and sorrow—that this was the best time of my life, and the only chance I would ever have of recapturing it, or even getting close to it, was by deploying with my rifle and my brothers. Nobody recognizes the best moment in life as it's happening. It takes distance and time to see. But once you do, it has a tremendous pull on your heart and your soul and your brain. To me, that's what the Balad deployment had become—and also what I was most afraid of, that my best years were behind me and that I'd be bored and unfulfilled the rest of my life as a result.

You might be thinking, "Mat, you were only twenty-nine years old, how could you possibly know that this will be the greatest moment of your life forever?" Honestly, I *didn't* know. I knew that the men I served with were the greatest men I've ever known. I knew that no matter how successful I got or how big Black Rifle Coffee grew or how great a place it was to work or how many veterans we hired or how amazing it felt to have found another brother who was as solid of a human as Evan Hafer is, I would never have that carefree feeling again, where nothing else in the world mattered except the soldiers on either side of me. I knew I would never get to be a twenty-three-year-old warfighting badass again. But that's life, right? The world turns and life moves forward. War ends.

Or does it?

I realized that the war we were sent to fight on behalf of America was not the only war we were fighting. Far from it. As veterans, we also fought millions of horrible individual wars within ourselves. My inner war was not with PTSD or survivor's guilt or regret or some weird kind of FOMO (fear of missing out). My war was with war. I was fighting an addiction to war.

War was my heroin and got me high unlike anything I had ever experienced. My needle was a gun, and I was shooting into the first vein I could find. What made those two years after leaving the Rangers so difficult for me was that I had quit war cold turkey and I was suffering from withdrawal.

At the time, I called it needing a purpose, which was half-true. What I really needed was a fix.

Thankfully, I had enough of my wits about me at the time to recognize that I could not go back in all the way. I could not commit 100 percent to chasing that dragon. It would drive me insane, and then it would kill me. By my fifth deployment, I already thought I was dead. Death just hadn't gotten the news. If I reenlisted, it would have been like sending him a text message with my picture in it. So instead, I became a contractor, which functioned more or less like my methadone. I got 80 percent of the high— enough to take the edge off—with enough mental clarity that my brain could recognize real opportunity and genuine purpose when it placed itself in front of me.

Article 15, Leadslingers, Black Rifle Coffee, *entrepreneurship*— that is real opportunity. Tapping into my love of music and my capacity for creativity; leveraging the leadership and team-building skills I learned in the Army; making great things that make a lot of people happy and helping veterans and their families in the process—that is genuine purpose. Being the person I always wanted to be without boundaries.

I pulled out my phone and dialed the contracting office.

"Hi, it's me, Mat Best. Yeah, I'm done."

——

When we got back to El Paso, I made an executive decision. I packed one bag full of guns and one suitcase full of clothes, threw them in the back of my truck, and drove 850 miles through the night to Salt Lake City where Evan lived, to relocate and commit fully to what we were building together at Black Rifle Coffee Company. Everything else I had in El Paso—all my shit, all my toys, old business, and the girlfriend I had been living with—I left all of it right where it was. It cost me, but it was still the best decision I could have made.

I know this not only because our coffee company started to get traction, but because Evan Hafer was in the hotel room in Colorado that night a year or so later, when I pushed all my chips into the middle of the table and cut the crap. He pushed all of his chips in as well. To be fair, he was already all-in, I was just catching up to him, but he understood what I was trying to say and do, and he was right there with me. Jarred too.

In the years after I walked away from the drug called war, I have relentlessly chased new dreams. It's been a hell of a ride. I mean, shit, here I am writing a book about my life. I even got married to a smart, talented, beautiful woman. On purpose! She has helped me crystallize the fact that making a difference in the lives of my military brothers and sisters has become my purpose in life, a purpose as great and as worthy as the one I tried hard to fulfill as a Ranger in 2/75.

I don't know how this story ends. I can only say, to all the brothers I've lost along the way, you are my motivation in everything I do. I'm thankful for every challenge we've faced together, and I look forward to those still to come. Every step (and misstep) we've taken has made me who I am today, and I refuse to live a life, to take another single step without you, that doesn't honor your sacrifice. It is the least I can do, because you have given the most.

My hope is that through my actions as a veteran and an entrepreneur, through the choices we make as a company, that we can inspire our community and show the next generation of veterans to never let anyone or anything stand in the way of their goals. It has been humbling for Evan, Jarred, and me, as veterans and as employers, to see what the remarkable men and women who serve this country can accomplish—not only in combat but also as they transition to the civilian sector and continue to serve this great nation with their effort, their energy, their loyalty, and their commitment to brotherhood.

Hardship paves the path to light. Be strong, be kind, be relentless, and always choose life.

Rangers lead the way.

Acknowledgments

Writing a book is really hard, especially when I was told I couldn't do it in crayon. It is humbling and exciting to be able to share my version of this crazy thing we call life. The fact that I'm not dead just means I'm on borrowed time and I'm thankful for every moment I have. I've been fortunate to share some extraordinary moments with amazing people. Here are a few of those amazing people that I couldn't have written this book without.

Nils Parker, your professionalism and writing are unmatched. The late night conversations, the last-minute flights to refine every aspect of this book, and your attention to detail about every part of my life truly don't go unnoticed. You have been a mentor through this whole process and I never could have done it without you. Your quick wit is continually impressive and frustrating.

Byrd Leavell, my agent, who helped me find the right place for this book, and who helped me figure out how to navigate my irreverence to make a style of book never read before.

Brendan Vaughan for having faith in the book even as it lingered in DoD review for almost two years. Pamela Cannon, Kara Welsh, and the entire team at Ballantine Bantam Dell for bringing it across the finish line and helping to get it into as many readers' hands as possible.

Jarred Taylor, for loving my first videos and having priorities that were just out of whack enough for us to get together and make the journey that led to this book even being possible.

Evan Hafer, for your faith in me as a business partner. Your drive motivates me every day to be a better human. #Bromance

Bobby Hill, the man that will make you look like $1 million and then cheer you on while you do mixed martial arts with a deer.

My brothers in 2/75: Serving with such quality and brave people will always be one of the highlights of my life. RLTW.

To my Dad, one of my best friends, I love you big bunches!

To my biological brothers, Davis and Alan, thank you for holding me down and shooting me with an airsoft gun as a kid. Oh yeah, and for pushing me over and telling our parents I slipped. I couldn't ask for better brothers, seriously. Love you, assholes.

And last but not least, to my wife, Noelle: how you put up with my craziness is not only impressive, but also just plain brave. Thank you for loving me unconditionally and having my back through this crazy journey.

About the Author

MAT BEST is a former U.S. Army Ranger serving with the 2nd Ranger Battalion, 75th Ranger Regiment. He was deployed five times to Iraq and Afghanistan, four times to Operation Iraqi Freedom and once to Operation Enduring Freedom as a fire team leader. He then spent five years working as a private military contractor. In 2012, Best created his first YouTube video, and his social media presence has since accumulated more than three million subscribers and fans while generating hundreds of millions of views. Best is also the co-founder of three successful businesses, Black Rifle Coffee, Leadslingers Whiskey, and Article 15 Clothing, and serves as executive vice president of Black Rifle Coffee. In addition, he co-produced the feature film *Range 15,* the most successful independent, crowd-funded film at the box office in the summer of 2016. Raised in Santa Barbara, California, and the youngest of six from a military family, Mat Best lives in San Antonio, Texas.

blackriflecoffee.com
Facebook.com/mbest11x
Twitter: @MatBest11x
Instagram: @mat_best_official
YouTube: @MBest11x

About the Type

This book was set in Aster, a typeface designed in 1958 by Francesco Simoncini (d. 1967). Aster is a round, legible face of even weight and was planned by the designer for the text setting of newspapers and books.